The BIG NORTH DAKOTA REPRODUCIBLE Activity Book!

BY CAROLE MARSH

This activity book has material that correlates with the
North Dakota Social Studies Content Standards.

At every opportunity, we have tried to relate information to
the North Dakota History and Social Science, English, Science,
Math, Civics, Economics, and Computer Technology directives.

For additional information, go to our websites:
www.northdakotaexperience.com or **www.gallopade.com**.

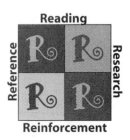

The Big Activity Book Team

Billie Walburn

Michael Marsh

Antoinette Miller

Michele Yother

Carole Marsh

Steven Saint-Laurent

Bob Longmeyer

Kathy Zimmer

Chad Beard

Cranston Davenport

Shery Kearney

Sherry Moss

Cecil Anderson

Pat Newman

Jackie Clayton

Terry Briggs

Victoria DeJoy

Al Fortunatti

Pam Dufresne

Permission is hereby granted to the individual purchaser or classroom teacher to reproduce materials in this book for non-commercial individual or classroom use only.

Reproduction of these materials for an entire school or school system is strictly prohibited.

Gallopade is proud to be a member of these educational organizations and associations:

Published by

GALLOPADE™
INTERNATIONAL
800-536-2GET
www.gallopade.com

SHOPA MEMBER™
School, Home, & Office Products Association

NSSEA

The North Dakota Experience Series

My First Pocket Guide to North Dakota!

The North Dakota Coloring Book!

My First Book About North Dakota!

North Dakota Jeopardy: Answers and Questions About Our State

North Dakota "Jography!": A Fun Run Through Our State

The North Dakota Experience! Sticker Pack

The North Dakota Experience! Poster/Map

Discover North Dakota CD-ROM

North Dakota "GEO" Bingo Game

North Dakota "HISTO" Bingo Game

A Word From The Author

North Dakota is a very special state. Almost everything about North Dakota is interesting and fun! It has a remarkable history that helped create the great nation of America. North Dakota enjoys an amazing geography of incredible beauty and fascination. The state's people are unique and have accomplished many great things.

This Activity Book is chock-full of activities to entice you to learn more about North Dakota. While completing puzzles, coloring activities, word codes, and other fun-to-do activities, you'll learn about your state's history, geography, people, places, animals, legends, and more.

Whether you're sitting in a classroom, stuck inside on a rainy day, or—better yet—sitting in the back seat of a car touring the wonderful state of North Dakota, my hope is that you have as much fun using this Activity Book as I did writing it.

Enjoy your North Dakota Experience—it's the trip of a lifetime!!

Carole Marsh

Geographic Tools

Beside each geographic need listed, put the initials of the tool that can best help you!

(CR) Compass Rose   (LL) Longitude and Latitude
(M) Map   (G) Grid
(K) Map key/legend

1. _____ I need to find the geographic location of Germany.

2. _____ I need to learn where an airport is located near Napoleon.

3. _____ I need to find which way is north.

4. _____ I need to chart a route from North Dakota to California.

5. _____ I need to find a small town on a map.

Match the items on the left with the items on the right.

1. Grid system
2. Compass rose
3. Longitude and latitude
4. Two of North Dakota's borders
5. Symbols on a map

A. Map key or legend
B. Montana and Minnesota
C. A system of letters and numbers
D. Imaginary lines around the earth
E. Shows N, S, E, and W

ANSWERS: 1-LL; 2-K; 3-CR; 4-M; 5-G; 1-C; 2-E; 3-D; 4-B; 5-A

The Badlands are Good for North Dakota!

The Theodore Roosevelt National Park in North Dakota's Badlands is the state's major tourist attraction. The brilliantly colored tablelands, buttes, petrified trees, colored clays, and conelike hills have changed very little since Theodore Roosevelt first visited the Badlands in 1883. The park is open year-round and offers camping, hiking, and designated walking and horse trails.

Visitors can get to know Teddy Roosevelt on their tour of the Badlands. The Maltese Cross Cabin was originally located on Roosevelt's first Badlands ranch-a partnership with two other men called the Maltese Cross Ranch. Roosevelt later started his own ranch in the Badlands, the Elkhorn Ranch. After both his wife and mother died within hours of each other, the grief-stricken Roosevelt retreated to his new home.

Animals living in the park include buffalo, elk, deer, coyotes, bobcats, badgers, beavers, and rabbits. The area became a national park in 1947.

Using the information above, answer the following questions:

1. What is the name of the national park located in North Dakota's Badlands?

_____

2. What were the names of the ranches Teddy Roosevelt owned in the Badlands?

_____

3. When is Theodore Roosevelt National Park open?

_____

4. What is the name of the cabin located on Teddy Roosevelt's first ranch in the Badlands?

_____

ANSWERS: (may vary slightly) 1–Theodore Roosevelt National Park; 2–Maltese Cross Ranch and Elkhorn Ranch; 3–all year-round; 4–Maltese Cross Cabin

North Dakota Government

North Dakota's state government, just like our national government, is made up of three branches. Each branch has a certain job to do. Each branch also has some power over the other branches. We call this system checks and balances. The three branches work together to make our government work smoothly.

North Dakota's legislature has two houses. The Senate has 53 members and the House of Representatives has 106 members.	The executive branch of government includes the governor, secretary of state, attorney general, auditor, treasurer, and superintendent of public instruction.	The North Dakota Supreme Court has five members. The Supreme Court supervises a unified judicial system of district, county, and municipal courts.
Legislative Branch	**Executive Branch**	**Judicial Branch**

For each of these government officials, circle whether he or she is part of the EXECUTIVE, the LEGISLATIVE, or the JUDICIAL branch

1. Supreme Court justice	EXECUTIVE	LEGISLATIVE	JUDICIAL
2. governor	EXECUTIVE	LEGISLATIVE	JUDICIAL
3. state senator	EXECUTIVE	LEGISLATIVE	JUDICIAL
4. state representative	EXECUTIVE	LEGISLATIVE	JUDICIAL
5. probate judge	EXECUTIVE	LEGISLATIVE	JUDICIAL
6. speaker of the house	EXECUTIVE	LEGISLATIVE	JUDICIAL
7. secretary of state	EXECUTIVE	LEGISLATIVE	JUDICIAL
8. attorney general	EXECUTIVE	LEGISLATIVE	JUDICIAL

The number of legislators may change after each census.

ANSWERS: 1-judicial; 2-executive; 3-legislative; 4-legislative; 5-judicial; 6-legislative; 7-executive; 8-executive

All Around North Dakota!
Bubblegram

Fill in the bubblegram by using the clues below.

1. A state south of North Dakota
2. A country that borders North Dakota
3. The capital city of North Dakota
4. A river in eastern North Dakota
5. A river in northeastern North Dakota
6. A state west of North Dakota
7. A mountain range in the north

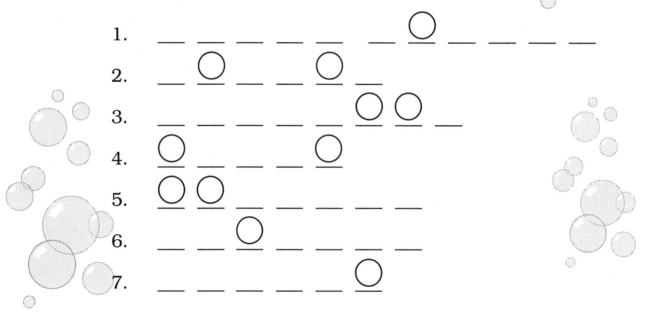

Now unscramble the "bubble" letters to find out the mystery words!
Hint: What is North Dakota's state nickname?

The __ __ __ __ __ __ __ __ __ __ __ state

Beautiful Bison

There was a time when as many as 60 million bison, also called buffalo, roamed North America! They are the largest wild animal in the United States. A bison bull (male) can be 6 feet (1.8 meters) tall, 10 feet (3 meters) long, and weigh over one ton (0.9 metric ton). A bison cow (female) is smaller. Both have horns. Bison were almost hunted to extinction! By the late 1880s, only a handful remained. The animals that remained were protected, and now bison number in the thousands!

Learn more about bison by figuring out the facts below.

1. Plains Indians in the  + AS depended on bison for

   food, + - R, + TER, and arrow points.

   _____ _____ _____

2. Plains 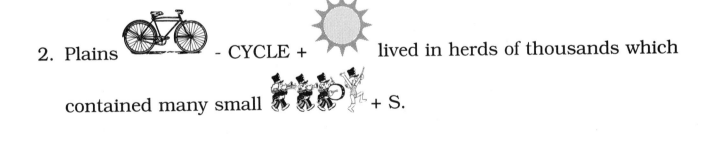 - CYCLE + lived in herds of thousands which

   contained many small + S.

   _____ _____

3. Bison are a  of wild + .

   _____ _____

North Dakota Wheel of Fortune, Indian Style!

The names of North Dakota's many Native American tribes contain enough consonants to play . . . Wheel of Fortune!

See if you can figure out the Wheel of Fortune-style puzzles below! "Vanna" has given you some of the consonants in each word.

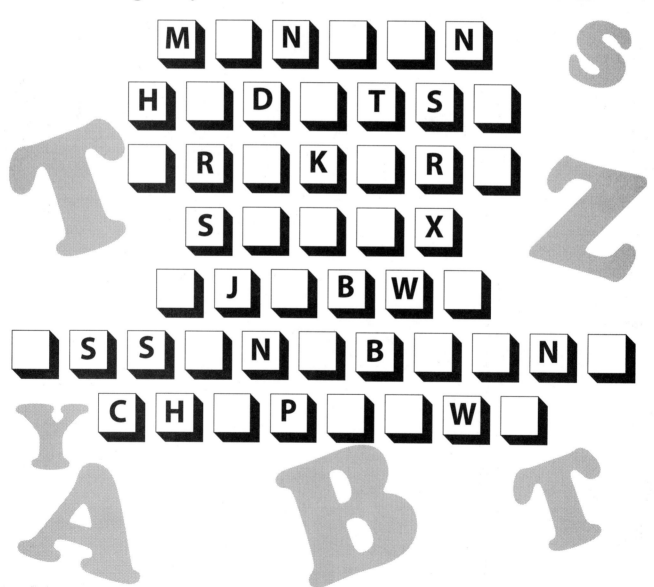

Rainbow, Pretty Rainbow

Rainbows often appear over Lake Sakakawea after a storm. Rainbows are formed when sunlight bends through raindrops. Big raindrops produce the brightest, most beautiful rainbows. You can see rainbows early or late on a rainy day when the sun is behind you.

Color the rainbow in the order the colors are listed below, starting at the top of the rainbow. Then, in each band write down as many North Dakota-related words as you can think of that begin with the same first letter as that color!

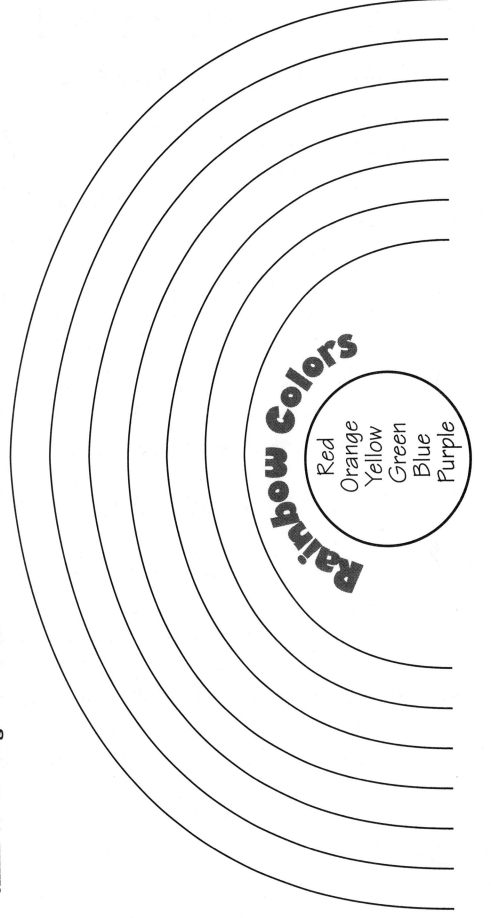

Rainbow Colors

Red
Orange
Yellow
Green
Blue
Purple

In the Beginning...
There Were the French

Fur trading and the search for a Northwest Passage (a water route connecting the Atlantic and Pacific oceans) brought the first explorers to North Dakota. Pierre Gaultier de Varennes, Sieur de La Vérendrye, was the first person to write about his travels and the Indians in North Dakota.

In 1797, the North West Company sent David Thompson to find their trading posts and determine if they were north or south of the 49th parallel (the U.S.-Canadian border). He was the first person to map part of North Dakota.

President Thomas Jefferson sent Meriwether Lewis and William Clark on an expedition to explore the lands the United States bought from France in the 1803 Louisiana Purchase. The explorers spent five months in North Dakota during the winter of 1804-1805.

Help the Lewis and Clark expedition find their way to the Little Missouri River!

Sakakawea, the Shoshone Indian woman who served Lewis and Clark as guide and interpreter, joined the expedition at Fort Mandan.

Finish

Little Missouri River

Start

U.S. Time Zones

Would you believe that the contiguous United States is divided into four time zones? It is! Because of the rotation of the earth, the sun appears to travel from east to west. Whenever the sun is directly overhead, we call that time noon. When it is noon in Atlanta, Georgia, the sun has a long way to go before it is directly over Bowman, North Dakota.

The contiguous United States has four different time zones. They are the Eastern time zone, the Central time zone, the Mountain time zone, and the Pacific time zone. There is a one-hour time difference between each zone!

North Dakota is split into two different time zones-the Mountain time zone and the Central time zone. When it is 12:00 p.m. (noon) Amidon, North Dakota, it is 1:00 p.m. in Fargo, North Dakota. When its is 9:00 p.m. in New England, North Dakota, it is 10:00 p.m. in Walhalla, North Dakota.

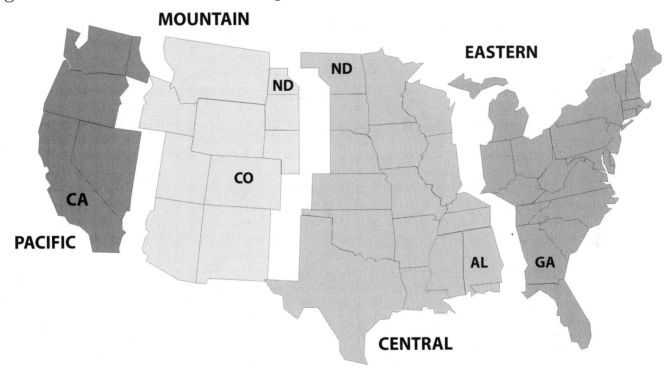

Look at the time zones on the map below then answer the following questions:

1. When it is 10:00 a.m. in Beach, North Dakota, what time is it in California? _____ a.m.
2. When it is 3:30 p.m. in Atlanta, Georgia, what time is it in Ellendale, North Dakota? _____ p.m.
3. In what time zone is North Dakota located? _____
4. In what time zone is Colorado located? _____
5. If it is 10:00 p.m. in Hope, North Dakota, what time is it in Alabama? _____ p.m.

ANSWERS: 1-9:00 a.m., 2-2:30 p.m.; 3-Central and Mountain; 4-Mountain; 5-10:00 p.m.

Sing Like a North Dakota Bird Word Jumble

Arrange the jumbled letters in the proper order for the names of birds found in North Dakota.

hungarian partridge

prairie chicken

mockingbird

white pelican

mourning dove

owl

western meadowlark

bobolink

blue heron

wild turkey

1. I N O K B O L B

   __ __ __ __ __ __ __ __

2. R P I I A E R   H C N I K C E

   __ __ __ __ __ __ __ __ __ __ __ __ __ __

3. H E T I W   C E L N P I A

   __ __ __ __ __   __ __ __ __ __ __ __

4. U L B E   E N H R O

   __ __ __ __   __ __ __ __ __

5. O M K I R C I B D N G

   __ __ __ __ __ __ __ __ __ __

6. I D L W   T K R Y E U

   __ __ __ __   __ __ __ __ __ __

7. N O M I N U R G   V O E D

   __ __ __ __ __ __ __ __   __ __ __ __

8. W O L

   __ __ __

9. S R N W E T E   K E A M W L D A O R

   __ __ __ __ __ __ __   __ __ __ __ __ __ __ __ __

10. A R U I A N H G N   G A R D R T P I E

   __ __ __ __ __ __ __ __ __   __ __ __ __ __ __ __ __ __

ANSWERS: 1–bobolink; 2–prairie chicken; 3–white pelican; 4–blue heron; 5– mockingbird; 6– wild turkey; 7–mourning dove; 8–owl; 9–western meadowlark; 10–hungarian partridge

©2001 Carole Marsh/Gallopade International/800-536-2GET/www.northdakotaexperience.com/Page 14

North Dakota Schools Rule!

The first school in North Dakota was a Catholic mission school attended by Métis (people of mixed Chippewa and European, usually French, descent) children. The school was established at Pembina before 1820. Public school systems were provided for soon after Dakota Territory was organized in 1861. Eleven students reported to class the day the University of North Dakota opened in Grand Forks in 1884. North Dakota State University in Fargo opened as the North Dakota Agricultural College in 1890. Schools that are part of North Dakota's state university system also include Valley City State University, Williston State College, Bismarck State College, Dickinson State University, Mayville State University, Minot State University, Lake Region State College in Devils Lake, and North Dakota State College of Science in Wahpeton.

Complete the names of these North Dakota schools. Use the Word Bank to help you. Then, use the answers to solve the code at the bottom.

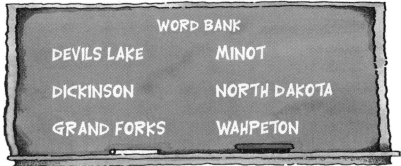

WORD BANK

DEVILS LAKE   MINOT

DICKINSON   NORTH DAKOTA

GRAND FORKS   WAHPETON

1. The University of North Dakota in

___ ___ ___ ___ ___ ___ ___ ___ ___ ___ ___
                              5

2. ___ ___ ___ ___ ___ ___ ___ ___ ___ ___ State University
   1

3. ___ ___ ___ ___ ___ ___ State University
   6

4. ___ ___ ___ ___ ___ ___ ___ ___ ___ ___ ___ State
                     7
   University in Fargo

5. North Dakota State College of Science in

___ ___ ___ ___ ___ ___ ___ ___
           3

6. Lake Region State College in

___ ___ ___ ___ ___ ___ ___ ___ ___ ___ ___
        2   4

The coded message tells you what all college students want!

___ ___ ___ ___ ___ ___ ___
1   2   3   4   5   6   7

North Dakota Topography is "Tops"!

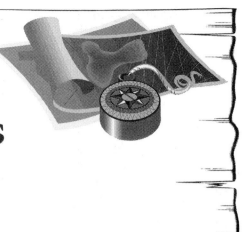

When we learn about North Dakota's topography, we use special words to describe it. These words describe the things that make each part of the state interesting.

Cross out every other letter below beginning with the first one to find out what each topographical term is!

1. F V G A S L O L P E Z Y
   a stretch of low land lying between hills or mountains

2. W G V L Y A H C K I J E F R
   a large mass of ice that moves very slowly down a mountain or across land until it melts

3. H M V O S U X N C T D A Z I E N P R O A B N H G Q E
   a group of mountains

4. G B W U C T X T P E
   a steep, flat-topped hill standing alone

5. J T F R E I H B S U Q T Z A K R L Y
   a stream or river that flows into a larger stream or river

6. V H D I Z G Y H Q L M A C N K D
   an area of hills or mountains higher than the land around it

7. M P V L E A Q I W N
   a flat area of land with few variations

8. W R V E K S A E B R L V G O H I Z R
   a natural or artificial place where water is collected and stored for use

9. B R Y A P V L I J N C E
   a gorge, a long deep hollow

10. R P W L V A K T U E M A S U
    a stretch of high, level land

Oh! Say Can You See...
The North Dakota State Flag

North Dakota's current state flag was adopted in 1911. It features a blue field with an eagle holding an olive branch, representing peace, and seven arrows representing war. The eagle holds a banner that says *E Pluribus Unum*, Latin for "Out of the Many, One," a phrase that refers to the many states that make up the United States.
Color the North Dakota flag.

FAST FACTS

State Representative Colonel John H. Fraine introduced the legislation for the North Dakota state flag. The legislation requires the flag to be the same color, size, and form of the regimental flag used by the North Dakota Infantry during the Spanish-American War in 1898 and the Philippine Island Insurrection in 1899.

The North Dakota legislature adopted the North Dakota state flag on March 3, 1911.

Design your own Diamante on North Dakota!

A *diamante* is a cool diamond-shaped poem on any subject.

You can write your very own diamante poem on North Dakota by following the simple line by line directions below. Give it a try!

Line 1:   Write the name of the state capital.

Line 2:   Write the name of the state.

Line 3:   Write the state nickname.

Line 4:   Write the name of the state march.

Line 5:   Write the name of the state flower.

Line 6:   Write the name of the state bird.

Line 7:   Write what the word *Dakota* means in Sioux

_____

_____ _____

_____   _____   _____

_____   _____   _____   _____

_____   _____   _____

_____   _____

_____

YOU'RE a poet! Did you know it?

History Mystery Tour!

North Dakota is bursting at the seams with history! Here are just a few of the many historical sites that you might visit. **Try your hand at locating them on the map! Draw the symbol for each site on the North Dakota map below.**

Fort Union Trading Post National Historic Site, near Williston—built by American Fur Company in 1829

Knife River Indian Village National Historic Site, near Stanton—site of several Mandan, Hidatsa, and Akira earth-lodge villages

Menoken Indian Village State Historic Site, near Bismarck—site of prehistoric earth-lodge village

Pembina State Historic Site—first permanent settlement in North Dakota

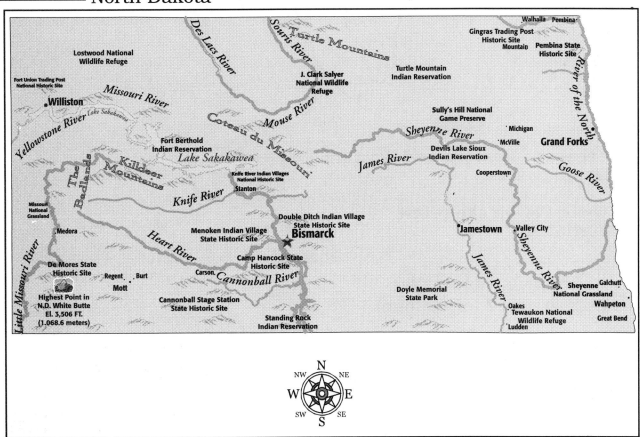

What in the World?

A hemisphere is one-half of a sphere (globe) created by the prime meridian or equator. Every place in the world is in two hemispheres (Northern or Southern and Eastern or Western). The equator is an imaginary line that runs around the world from left to right and divides the globe into the Northern Hemisphere and the Southern Hemisphere. The prime meridian is an imaginary line that runs around the world from top to bottom and divides the globe into the Eastern Hemisphere and Western Hemisphere.

Label the Northern and Southern Hemispheres.

Write E on the equator.

Is North Dakota in the NORTHERN or SOUTHERN Hemisphere? (circle one)

Color the map.

Label the Eastern and Western Hemispheres.

Write PM on the prime meridian.

Is North Dakota in the EASTERN or WESTERN Hemisphere? (circle one)

Color the map.

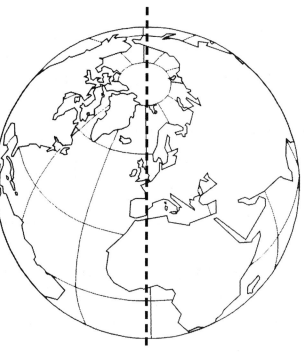

Places to go! Things to do!

North Dakota has so many cool places to go and so many cool things to do! **Use the Word Bank to help you complete the sentences below and learn about some of the exciting North Dakota sites you can visit!**

1. __ __ __ __ __ __ __ __ Roosevelt National Park in western North Dakota covers 70,000 acres (28,328 hectares) of badlands and prairie along the Little Missouri River.

2. Bonanzaville, USA, in __ __ __ __ __ is a restored pioneer village.

3. Salem Sue near __ __ __ __ __ __ __ __ __ is the world's largest Holstein cow replica.

4. The World's Largest Buffalo in

   __ __ __ __ __ __ __ __ is a three-story, 60-ton (54-metric ton) concrete buffalo sculpture.

5. __ __ __ __ __ __ __ __ __ Park Zoo in Minot is home to a black-footed penguin collection.

6. Exhibits of antique dolls and toys are on display at the __ __ __ __ __ __ Doll House.

7. Exhibits and hands-on demonstrations can be found at the Children's Museum at __ __ __ __ __ __ Farm in Fargo.

8. North Dakota Sports Hall of Fame in

   __ __ __ __ __ __ __ __ __ honors those who helped develop sports in the state.

WORD BANK

Dickinson	Jamestown	Medora	Theodore
Fargo	Jamestown	Roosevelt	Yunker

ANSWERS: 1–Theodore; 2–Fargo; 3–Dickinson; 4–Jamestown; 5–Roosevelt; 6–Medora; 7–Yunker; 8–Jamestown

Please Come to North Dakota!

You have a friend who lives in New Hampshire. She is thinking of moving to North Dakota because she wants to be a rodeo clown, and North Dakota's cities and towns hold about 50 rodeos every year.

Write her a letter describing North Dakota and some of the rodeo clown opportunities there.

There are four types of rodeos held in North Dakota-high school, college, amateur, and professional. North Dakota hosts all kinds of rodeo events from a "showdeo" for children to the Professional Rodeo Association. One of the most popular rodeos is the Rough Rider Days Rodeo held in Dickinson every year on the Fourth of July weekend. Dickinson is known as the "rodeo capital of North Dakota."

Naturally North Dakota!

North Dakota has many natural wonders! North Dakota Burning Coal Vein, north of Amidon, is a badlands landscape still being formed. Fire, which may have started by a lightning strike hundreds of years ago, smolders in the coal layer located several feet underground. The "stairstep" appearance is caused when the coal becomes ash and the clay above it cracks and falls into the fire.

Pembina Gorge, near Walhalla, is a forest valley formed by glacial meltwaters. The gorge includes forests, shrublands, prairies, and wetlands. It is home to a herd of elk, more than 75 species of birds, and more than 480 plant species.

1. Pembina Gorge is located near _____. (ACROSS)
2. North Dakota Burning Coal Vein is a _____ landscape still being formed. (DOWN)
3. North Dakota Burning Coal Vein's "stairstep" appearance is caused when the coal becomes _____. (DOWN)
4. The underground fire at North Dakota Burning Coal Vein probably started because of a _____ strike. (DOWN)
5. North Dakota Burning Coal Vein is located north of _____. (ACROSS)
6. Pembina _____ was formed by glacial meltwaters. (ACROSS)

ANSWERS: 1—Walhalla; 2—badlands; 3—ash; 4—lightning; 5—Amidon; 6—Gorge

North Dakota Rules!

Use the code to complete the sentences.

A	B	C	D	E	F	G	H	I	J	K	L	M	N	O	P
1	2	3	4	5	6	7	8	9	10	11	12	13	14	15	16

Q	R	S	T	U	V	W	X	Y	Z
17	18	19	20	21	22	23	24	25	26

1. State rules are called __ __ __ __.
                 12 1 23 19

2. Laws are made in our state __ __ __ __ __ __ __.
             3 1 16 9 20 15 12

3. The leader of our state is the __ __ __ __ __ __ __ __.
           7 15 22 5 18 14 15 18

4. We live in the state of
   __ __ __ __ __   __ __ __ __ __ __1
   14 15 18 20 8   4 1 11 15 20 1

5. The capital of our state is __ __ __ __ __ __ __ __
           2 9 19 13 1 18 3 11

N O R T H
D A K O T A ! ! !

Buzzing Around North Dakota!

Write the answers to the questions below. To get to the beehive, follow a path through the maze.

1. North Dakota State Historical Museum is in _____.

2. _____ _____ is home to the University of North Dakota Zoology Museum.

3. The Geographical _____ Historical Museum is in Rugby.

4. The Turtle Mountain Chippewa Heritage Center is in _____.

5. _____ is home to the Lewis and Clark Trail Museum.

6. Frontier Museum in _____ resembles a turn-of-the-twentieth-century town.

7. Dinosaur bones found in North Dakota are featured at the Dakota Dinosaur Museum in _____.

8. North Dakota's largest collection of antique farm machinery is found at the Dale and Martha Hawk Foundation Museum in _____.

9. Exotic rocks and minerals from all over the world are found at the Broste Rock Museum in _____.

10. The North Dakota State Railroad Museum is in _____.

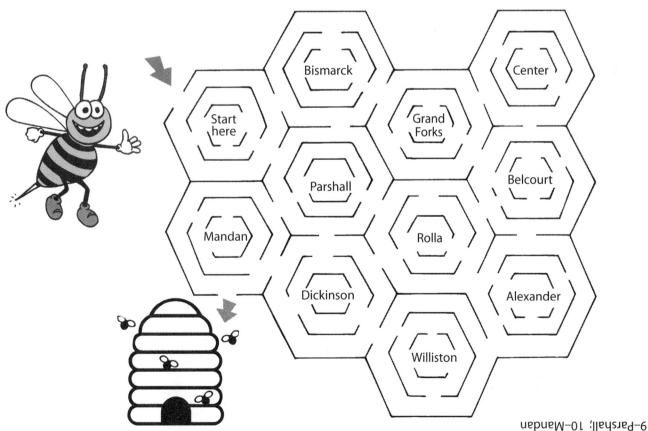

CALENDAR

North Dakota Through the Years!

Many great things have happened in North Dakota throughout its history. Chronicle the following important North Dakota events by solving math problems to find out the years in which they happened.

1. Pierre Gaultier de Varennes, Sieur de La Vérendrye, is the first person to write an account of his travels through North Dakota

   $1 \div 1 =$ $8-1 =$ $2+1 =$ $4 \times 2 =$

2. Alexander Henry, the Younger, establishes trading post at Pembina for the North West Company

   $2 \div 2 =$ $9-1 =$ $1 \times 0 =$ $1+0 =$

3. International Peace Garden is dedicated

   $3 \div 3 =$ $3 \times 3 =$ $4-1 =$ $1+1 =$

4. Bismarck becomes capital of the Dakota Territory

   $4 \div 4 =$ $4+4 =$ $6+2 =$ $6-3 =$

5. The United States buys the Louisiana Purchase territory, which includes parts of North Dakota, from France

   $5 \div 5 =$ $7+1 =$ $0 \times 4 =$ $4-1 =$

6. Theodore Roosevelt National Park is created

   $6 \div 6 =$ $7+2 =$ $2 \times 2 =$ $9-2 =$

7. Meriwether Lewis and William Clark Expedition builds winter quarters in North Dakota and hires Toussaint Charbonneau and his wife, Sakakawea, as guides

   $7 \div 7 =$ $3+5 =$ $0 \times 5 =$ $5-1 =$

8. A treaty with Great Britain gives the United States the rest of present-day North Dakota

   $8 \div 8 =$ $9-1 =$ $5-4 =$ $1+7 =$

9. Enabling Act divides Dakota Territory into two states; North Dakota admitted to the Union as the 39th state

   $9 \div 9 =$ $8-0 =$ $8 \times 1 =$ $9 \times 1 =$

10. Voter registration law is repealed; North Dakota becomes only state without this requirement

   $9-8 =$ $8+1 =$ $6-1 =$ $8-7 =$

ANSWERS: 1-1738; 2-1801; 3-1932; 4-1883; 5-1803; 6-1947; 7-1804; 8-1818; 9-1889; 10-1951

What Did We Do Before Money?

In early North Dakota, there were no banks. However, people still wanted to barter, trade, or otherwise "purchase" goods from each other. Wampum, made of shells, bone, or stones, was often swapped for goods. Indians, especially, used wampum for "money." In the barter system, people swapped goods or services.

Later, banks came into existence, and people began to use money to buy goods. However, they also still bartered when they had no money to spend.

Place a star in the box below the systems used today.

Rhymin' Riddles

1. I served as family doctor to the 16th president, then managed his re-election campaign;
   In return, the first territorial governor of North Dakota I became.

   Who am I? _____

2. I was a pioneer in the fur trade;
   In 1868, North Dakota's first homestead claim I made.

   Who am I? _____

3. I was a musician and entertainer who played the accordion;
   For 20 years, my show was popular on television;

   Who am I? _____

4. On the Red River, I was steamboat captain and flatboat operator;
   I helped found Grand Forks, then became its mayor.

   Who am I? _____

 # Map Symbols

Make up symbols for these names and draw them in the space provided on the right.

railroad	
airport	
cattle	
wheat	
poultry	
hospital	
oil	
fort	

North Dakota Goodies!

Match the name of each crop or product from North Dakota with the picture of that item.

Spring wheat   Sunflowers   Honey
Durum wheat   Pinto beans   Barley

 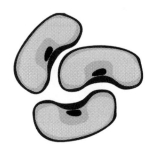 

FAST FACTS

Spring wheat is used for making bread flour.

North Dakota produces most of the nation's durum wheat, the main ingredient in pasta.

Agriculture has always played an important role in North Dakota's economy.

The top three small grains grown in North Dakota are durum wheat, spring wheat, and barley.

Barley is used for feeding livestock and brewing beer.

Historical North Dakota Women World Wonders!

North Dakota has been the home of many brave and influential women. See if you can match these women with their accomplishments.

1. Brynhild Haugland
2. Era Bell Thompson
3. Sakakawea
4. Anne Carlsen
5. Elizabeth Bodine
6. Peggy Lee
7. Angie Dickinson
8 Phyllis Frelich

a. named North Dakota Mother of the Year in 1968; all 18 of her children received post-high school education

b. singer, lyricist, composer and musical innovator; her hits include "Big Spender," "Fever," and "Is That All There Is?"

c. Shoshone Indian woman who joined the Lewis and Clark expedition in North Dakota and served as a guide and interpreter

d. actress; best-known for the movie *Dressed to Kill* and the television series *Police Woman*

e. politician; served as North Dakota legislator for 50 years

f. prominent African-American journalist, editor of *Ebony* magazine from 1951-1970

g. Tony Award-winning actress; founding member of the National Theater of the Deaf

h. brought national recognition to the Crippled Children's School in Jamestown, which is now named for her, while serving as the school's superintendent

ANSWERS: 1-e; 2-f; 3-c; 4-h; 5-a; 6-b; 7-d; 8-g

Producers and Consumers

Producers (sellers) make goods or provide services. Ralph, a fourth grade student in Montpelier, is a consumer because he wants to buy a new wheel for his bicycle. Other products and services from North Dakota that consumers can buy include animal feeds and fertilizer, farm machinery, dairy products, and oil and natural gas.

Complete these sentences.

Without dairy products, I couldn't

_____

_____

Without fertilizer, I couldn't

_____

_____

Without oil, I couldn't

_____

_____

Without farm machinery, I couldn't

_____

_____

North Dakota Word Wheel!

Use the Word Wheel of North Dakota names to complete the sentences below.

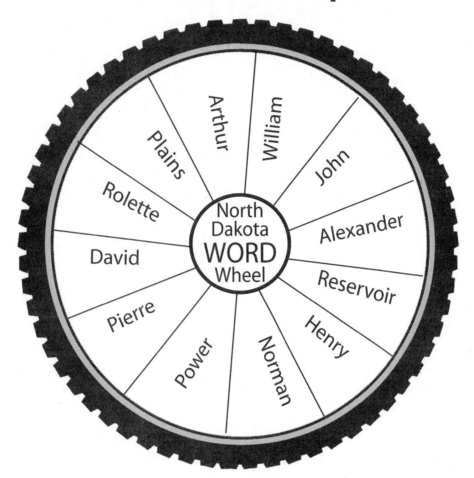

1. Robert _____ Bahmer was head of the National Archives and Records Administration.
2. _____ Bottineau was a Métis leader in the Red River Valley and led many expeditions across the northern plains.
3. _____ Kittson was a Pembina fur trader who became the first postmaster of North Dakota.
4. James B. _____ was called the "father of bonanza farming."
5. _____ Thompson made the first map of North Dakota.
6. _____ C. Townley was founder and president of the Nonpartisan League.
7. Joseph P. _____, Jr., filed the first homestead claim in North Dakota.
8. _____ McKenzie controlled business and politics in North Dakota from the 1880s–1906.
9. _____ Burke served North Dakota as a state senator, three-term governor, and as justice of the state supreme court.
10. _____ Lemke served North Dakota as a U.S. representative and ran for president in 1936

ANSWERS: 1–Henry; 2–Pierre; 3–Norman, 4–Power; 5–David; 6–Arthur; 7–Rolette; 8–Alexander; 9–John, 10–William

A Surplus of State Historic Sites!

North Dakota has lots of interesting state historic sites. You and your family decide to visit them. Decide which direction to travel from one site to the next.

1. **The tour starts in Bismarck at the Camp Hancock State Historic Site**. It was originally built as Camp Greeley in 1872 to protect the workers building the Northern Pacific Railroad. Your next stop is the **Cannonball Stage Station State Historic Site** near Carson. _____

2. The **Cannonball Stage Station State Historic Site** marks a stop on the Black Hills Trail. Your next stop is the **De Mores State Historic Site** located southwest of Medora. Which way do you go from Carson? _____

3. The **De Mores State Historic Site** honors Antoine de Vallombrosa, the Marquis de Mores. From Medora, you need to go to the **Double Ditch Indian Village State Historic Site** located a few miles north of Bismarck. Which way do you go? _____

4. After the **Double Ditch Indian Village State Historic Site** you want to journey to the **Gingras Trading Post State Historic Site**, the home and trading post of Métis trader Antoine B. Gingras. Which way do you travel to get from Bismarck to Walhalla? _____

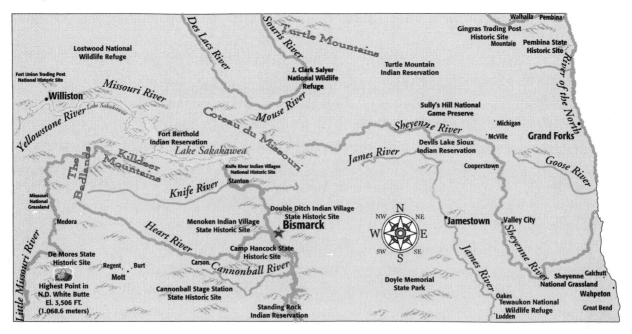

Create Your Own North Dakota State Quarter!

Look at the change in your pocket. You might notice that one of the coins has changed. The United States is minting new quarters, one for each of the 50 states. Each quarter has a design on it that says something special about one particular state. The North Dakota quarter will be in cash registers and piggy banks everywhere after it's released in 2006.

What if you had designed the North Dakota quarter? Draw a picture of how you would like the North Dakota quarter to look. Make sure you include things that are special about North Dakota.

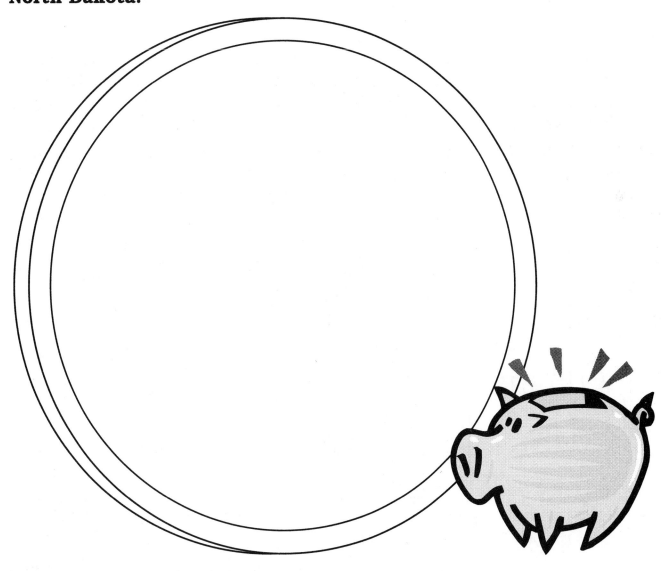

North Dakota Law Comes In Many Flavors!

For each of these people, write down the kind(s) of law used to decide whether their actions are legal or illegal.

1. Bank robber _____

2. Business person _____

3. State park ranger _____

4. North Dakotans _____

5. Doctor _____

6. Real estate agent _____

7. Corporate president _____

8. Ship owner _____

9. Diplomat _____

10. Soldier _____

Medical Law

International Law

Military Law

Commercial Law

Maritime Law

Antitrust Law

Environmental Law

Property Law

Criminal Law

State Law

ANSWERS: (Answers may vary) 1–Criminal; 2–Commercial; 3–Environmental; 4–State; 5–Medical; 6–Property; 7–Antitrust; 8–Maritime; 9–International; 10–Military

Mixed-Up States!

My friends are all mixed up! See if you can help them find their way back home!

Color, cut out, and paste each of North Dakota's three neighbors onto the map below.

Be sure and match the state shapes!

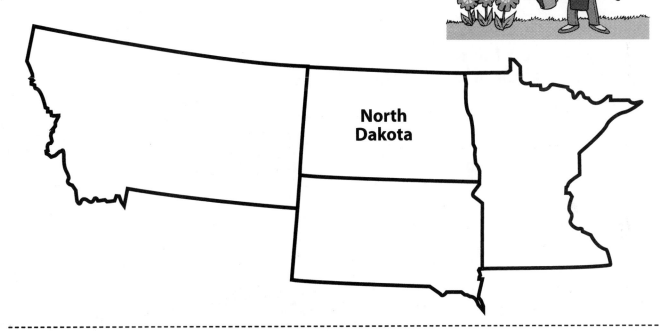

USS *North Dakota*

The USS *North Dakota*, a U.S. Navy battleship, was commissioned in 1910 and operated with the Atlantic Fleet along the East Coast and in the Caribbean. During the summers of 1912 and 1913, midshipmen from the U.S. Naval Academy were aboard the *North Dakota* for training. When political disturbances in Mexico threatened American citizens and interests 1914, the *North Dakota* spent seven months cruising Mexico's coast. During World War I, the Navy trained gunners and engineers on the *North Dakota*. During the summer of 1921, the *North Dakota* participated in the Army-Navy bombing tests off the Virginia coast in which the German warships *Frankfurt* and *Ostfriesland* were sunk to show the potential of airpower. The *North Dakota* spent more time training future naval officers before she was decommissioned in 1923.

When you're on board any kind of boat, you have to use special terms to talk about directions. Label the ship below with these terms:

bow:	front of the ship	**aft**:	towards the stern
stern:	back of the ship	**port**:	left as you face the bow
fore:	towards the bow	**starboard**:	right as you face the bow

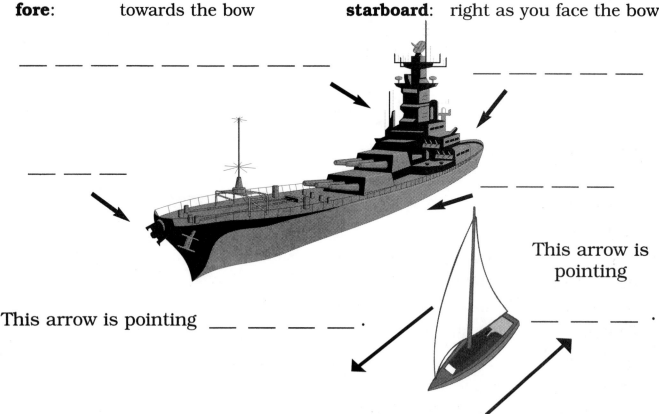

This arrow is pointing

This arrow is pointing __ __ __ __ .

__ __ __ __ .

North Dakota Politics As Usual!

Our elected government officials decide how much money is going to be spent on schools, roads, public parks, and libraries. Every election is important, and everyone who is eligible (able) to vote should do so!

Today, many elected government officials are women. However, before the 19th Amendment to the U.S. Constitution, women were unable to vote in national elections! A woman's suffrage bill was signed into law in 1917 in North Dakota. It was ratified in 1919 and women were able to vote in the 1920 general election. In 1920, enough states ratified the 19th Amendment, and it became the law of the land. Women gained suffrage nationally and continue to be a major force in the election process today.

On the lines provided, write down a question for each of the answers below. A hint follows each answer.

1. Question: _____

    Answer: A draft of a law presented for review.

    (Short for William!)

2. Question: _____

    Answer: The right to vote.

    (Don't make us suffer!)

3. Question: _____

    Answer: The ability to forbid a bill or law from being passed.

    (Just say no!)

4. Question: _____

    Answer: The fundamental law of the United States that was

    framed in 1787 and put into effect in 1789.

    (North Dakota has one too!)

5. Question: _____

    Answer: An amendment.

    (It's not something subtracted from #5!)

ANSWERS: (may vary slightly) 1–What is a bill? 2–What is suffrage? 3–What is a veto? 4–What is the Constitution? 5–What is an addition to the Constitution called?

What Shall I Be When I Grow Up?

Here are just a few of the jobs that kept early North Dakotans busy.

Lawyer
Tenant Farmer
Judge
Housekeeper
Silversmith
Politician
Dairyman
Wheelwright
Teacher
Cabinetmaker
Mayor
Cooper (barrelmaker)
Carpenter

Weaver
Barber
Gardener
Mantuamaker
(dressmaker)
Printer
Cook
Musician
Bookbinder
Laundress
Jeweler
Innkeeper
Stablehand

Tailor
Baker
Pharmacist
Gaoler (jailer)
Doctor
Governor
Milliner (hatmaker)
Soldier
Hunter
Blacksmith
Beekeeper
Gunsmith
Prospector

You are a young settler trying to decide what you want to be when you grow up. Choose a career and next to it write a description of what you think you would do each day as a:

Write your career choice here!

_____

Write your career choice here!

_____

Write your career choice here!

_____

Write your career choice here!

_____

Governor of North Dakota!

The governor is the leader of the state.

You've been assigned to write a biography of the governor of North Dakota.

Before you can start your book, you need to jot down some notes in your trusty computer. Fill in the necessary information in the spaces provided on the dossier!

GOVERNOR'S NAME:

_____

_____

Date of Birth: _____

Place of Birth: _____

Father: _____

Mother: _____

Siblings: _____

Spouse: _____

Children: _____

Pets: _____

Schools Attended: _____

_____

Previous Occupation(s): _____

_____

Likes: _____

_____

Dislikes: _____

_____

abc • APPLICATIONS   MENU   CALCULATOR   FIND   123 •

The ORIGINAL North Dakota Natives!

The Mandans were the first Indians to make their home in North Dakota. They lived in villages along the Missouri River and farmed. The Hidatsas and Arikaras also lived in villages and built permanent earth-lodge houses.

The Chippewas moved to North Dakota from Minnesota and settled in the forest areas of the Turtle Mountains.

Settlers and other Indian tribes feared the Sioux, the largest tribe in North Dakota. They had a highly structured and democratic nation, which had seven political divisions. They called themselves *Oceti Sakowin* (Seven Council Fires).

What kinds of things did Native Americans use in their everyday life? For each of the things shown, circle YES if Native Americans did use it, or NO if they didn't.

yes   no

yes   no

yes   no

yes   no

yes   no

yes   no

yes   no

yes   no

North Dakota States All Around Code-Buster!

Decipher the code and write in the names of the states that border North Dakota.

A	B	C	D	E	F	G	H	I	J	K	L	M	N	O	P	Q	R
✹	❁	✣	♣	➸	❤	❢	✲	✄	✆	☛	✈	✉	✿	☆	✦	✡	✐

S	T	U	V	W	X	Y	Z
❦	☎	➻	✶	✖	✍	✠	✓

1. ✉✄✿✿➸❦☆☎✹

2. ❦☆➻☎✲ ♣✹☛☆☎✹

3. ✉☆✿☎✹✿✹

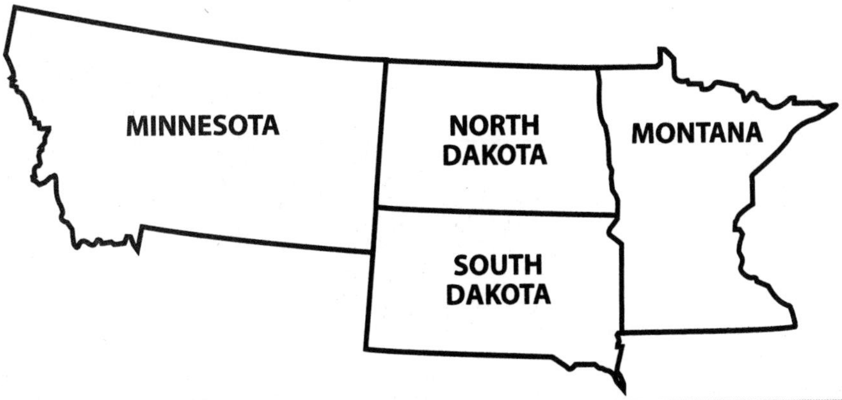

ANSWERS: 1-Minnesota; 2-South Dakota; 3-Montana

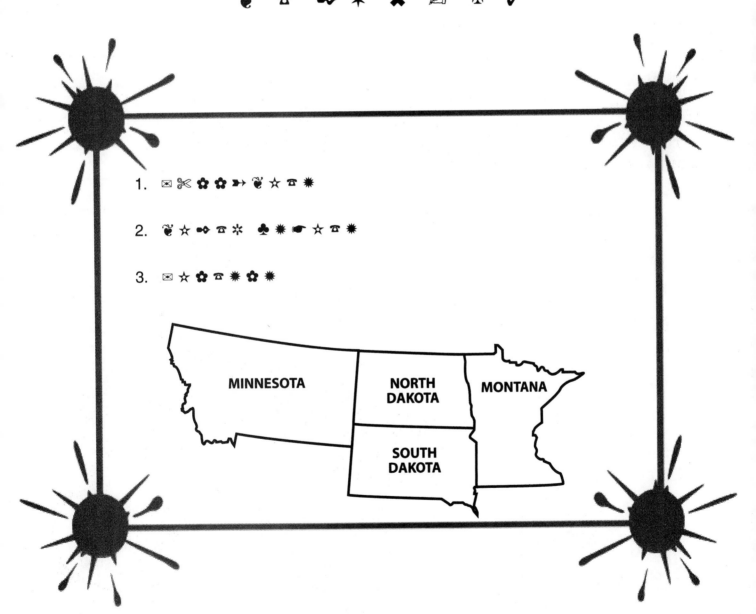

Unique North Dakota Place Names!

Can you figure out the compound words that make up the names of these North Dakota places?

Bathgate   _____   _____

Battleview   _____   _____

Bonetrail   _____   _____

Briarwood   _____   _____

Fairmount   _____   _____

Gladstone   _____   _____

Goodrich   _____   _____

Killdeer   _____   _____

Lawton   _____   _____

Northgate   _____   _____

Portland   _____   _____

Rocklake   _____   _____

Silverleaf   _____   _____

Starkwood   _____   _____

Underwood   _____   _____

Looking For a Home in North Dakota!

Can you figure out where these things, people, and animals belong? Use the word clues to help you!

1. Sullys Hill National Game Preserve, near (the spirit that represents evil + s) Lake, is home to buffalo, elk, deer and (liquid found in lakes and rivers + another name for bird).

   _____

   _____

2. (The name of what is shot from a bow + the hard part found under the bark of a tree or shrub) National Wildlife Refuge, near Jamestown, is home to duck broods in the summer and migrating geese in the fall.

   _____

3. (To pursue or run after someone) Lake National (something that lives or grows in nature + the quality that makes it possible for plants and animals to take in water, to eat, to grow) Refuge, near Medina, is home to the largest white pelican breeding colony in North America.

   _____

   _____

4. The Theodore Roosevelt National Park is home to (a prefix that means two + a boy or man as he is called by his parents), elk, and (a large level area of rolling grassland) dogs.

   _____

   _____

ANSWERS: 1–Devils, waterfowl; 2–Arrowwood; 3–Chase, Wildlife; 4–bison, prairie

I Love North Dakota, Weather or Not!

North Dakota has a continental climate, which means the state has four different seasons, fast temperature changes, low humidity, and a limited amount of rain.

North Dakota's temperatures can drop to 14°F (-10°C) in the winter and reach 73°F (23°C) in the summer. The highest temperature on record for North Dakota is 121°F (49°C) at Steele on July 6, 1936. The lowest temperature recorded in North Dakota is -60°F (-51°C) at Parshall on February 15, 1936.

FAST FACTS

The sun shines more than 15 hours a day from mid-May to July in North Dakota.

Spring floods hit 23 of North Dakota's 53 counties in 1979.

On the thermometer gauges below, color the mercury red (°F) to show the hottest temperature ever recorded in North Dakota. Color the mercury blue (°F) to show the coldest temperature ever recorded in North Dakota.

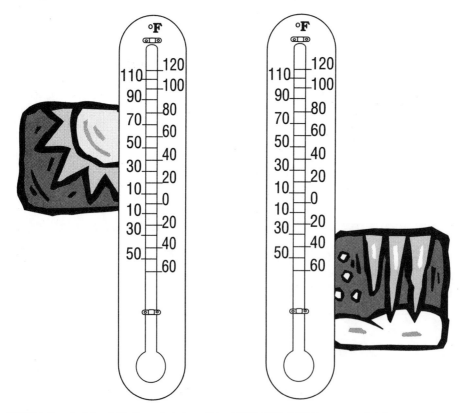

The Scenic Route

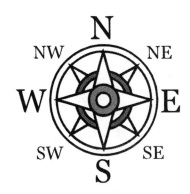

Imagine that you've planned an exciting exploratory expedition around North Dakota for your classmates. You've chosen some cities and other places to take your friends.

Circle these sites and cities on the map below, then number them in the order you would visit if you were traveling north to south through the state:

_____ Cooperstown

_____ Ludden

_____ McVille

_____ Michigan

_____ Mountain

_____ Oakes

_____ Valley City

_____ Walhalla

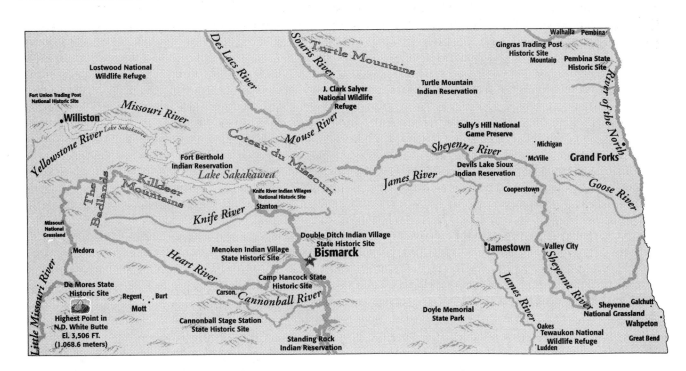

Key to a Map!

A map key, also called a map legend, shows symbols which represent different things on a map.

Match each word with a symbol for things found in the state of North Dakota.

airport **(Hector International Airport)**

church **(St. Mary's Catholic Church in Richardton)**

mountains **(White Butte)**

railroad **(Burlington Northern Santa Fe Railroad)**

river **(Red River of the North)**

road **(I-94)**

school **(University of North Dakota)**

state capital **(Bismarck)**

battle site **(Whitestone Hill Battlefield, near Kulm)**

bird sanctuary **(Chase Lake National Wildlife Refuge near Medina)**

BROTHER,
CAN YOU SPARE A DIME?

After the collapse of the stock market on Wall Street in 1929, the state of North Dakota, along with the rest of the nation, plunged headfirst into the Great Depression. It was the worst economic crisis America had ever known. Banks closed and businesses crashed...there was financial ruin everywhere.

Our President Helps

While the nation was in the midst of the Depression, Franklin Delano Roosevelt became president. With America on the brink of economic devastation, the federal government stepped forward and hired unemployed people to build parks, bridges, and roads. With this help, and other government assistance, the country began to slowly, and painfully, pull out of the Great Depression. Within the first 100 days of his office, Roosevelt enacted a number of policies to help minimize the suffering of the nation's many unemployed workers. These programs were known as the NEW DEAL. The jobs helped families support themselves and improved the country's infrastructure.

Low farm prices had already caused problems in North Dakota in the 1920s. When the Depression, combined with a drought, hit in the 1930s, North Dakota was nearly destroyed. Nearly one-third of North Dakota's farmers lost their property during the Depression. President Franklin Roosevelt's New Deal programs saved the state. The programs let farmers refinance their land, raised crop prices, and brought electricity to rural North Dakota.

Put an X next to the jobs that were part of Roosevelt's New Deal.

1. computer programmer _____

2. bridge builder _____

3. fashion model _____

4. park builder _____

5. interior designer _____

6. hospital builder _____

7. school builder _____

8. website designer _____

ANSWERS: 2 4 6 7

North Dakota Newcomers!

     People have come to North Dakota from other states and many other countries on almost every continent! As time goes by, North Dakota's population grows more diverse. This means that people of different races and from different cultures and ethnic backgrounds have moved to North Dakota.

     In the past, many immigrants have come to North Dakota from Norway, Germany, Russia, England, Ireland, Scotland, Wales, Sweden, and Denmark. More recently, people have migrated to North Dakota from Hispanic countries such as Mexico, as well as India and Asia. Only a certain number of immigrants are allowed to move to America each year. Many of these immigrants eventually become U.S. citizens.

Read the statement and decide if it's a fact or an opinion. Write your answer on the line.

1. Many of North Dakota's early immigrants came from Europe.
   _____

2. Lots of immigrants speak a language other than English.
   _____

3. The clothing immigrants wear is very interesting.
   _____

4. Immigrants from Norway have a neat accent when they speak.
   _____

5. Many immigrants will become United States citizens.
   _____

6. People have immigrated to North Dakota from nearly every country in the world.
   _____

An immigrant is a person who migrates to another country in hopes of a better life.

ANSWERS: 1-fact; 2-fact; 3-opinion; 4-opinion; 5-fact; 6-fact

A Day in the Life of a Settler

Pretend you are a settler in the days of early North Dakota. You keep a diary of what you do each day. Write in the "diary" what you might have done on a long, hot summer day in July 1873.

_____

_____

_____

_____

_____

_____

_____

_____

_____

_____

_____

_____

_____

_____

_____

This Old House!

Take yourself back 100 years. Can you imagine what life would be like in the Victorian Era? What did turn-of-the-century North Dakotans own? How did they live?

See if you can pick out which of the following items people at the turn of the century had and which ones they did not.

Circle the things you might find or use around your 1900 home.

Home, Sweet Home!

North Dakota has been the home of many different authors. Here are just a few. See if you can locate their hometowns on the map of North Dakota below! Write the number of each author near the town where he or she lived. Some towns may be used twice.

1. **Louis L'Amour** was born in a town west of Valley City and south of the Arrowwood National Wildlife Refuge. A western author, L'Amour published 88 novels including *Hondo* and *The Sacketts*.

2. **Louise Erdrich's** novels focus on what happens when white and Indians worlds meet. Her novels include *Love Medicine, Tracks*, and *The Beet Queen*. She was raised in a town located between Great Bend and Galchutt near the Minnesota state line.

3. **Jane Kurtz** has written 13 books, most of which are fiction for young readers. She lives in one of North Dakota's largest cities located on the Minnesota state line. Her books include *Fire on the Mountain, Trouble*, and *I'm Sorry, Almira Ann*.

4. Playwright **Maxwell Anderson** grew up in the same town as Louis L'Amour and graduated from the University of North Dakota. His plays include *The White Desert, What Price Glory?* with Laurence Stallings, and the Pulitzer Prize-winning *Both Your Houses*.

5. **Kathleen Eagle** taught for 17 years on this Indian reservation that is located in both North and South Dakota. She has written 38 romance novels, including *Someday Soon* which won the Romance Writers of America's Golden Heart Award in 1984.

6. **Larry Woiwode** is North Dakota's poet laureate, and he lives on a ranch between Regent and Burt in southwestern North Dakota. His books include *Born Brothers, Indian Affairs*, and *Even Tide*, a book of poetry.

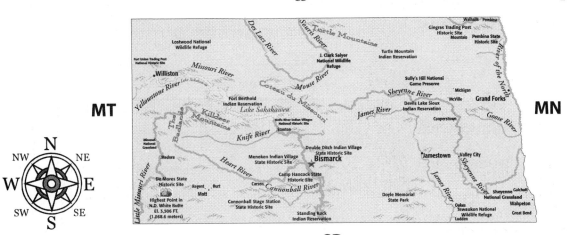

ANSWERS: 1—Jamestown; 2—Wahpeton; 3—Grand Forks; 4—Jamestown; 5—Standing Rock Indian Reservation; 6—Mott

North Dakota Spelling Bee!

Good spelling is a good habit. Study the words on the left side of the page. Then fold the page in half and "take a spelling test" on the right side. Have a buddy read the words aloud to you. When finished, unfold the page and check your spelling. Keep your score. GOOD LUCK.

Each word is worth 5 points.

agriculture _____

bonanza _____

buffalo _____

butte _____

conservation _____

Dakota _____

expedition _____

frontier _____

heritage _____

Missouri _____

Pembina _____

plains _____

prairie _____

rendezvous _____

reservoir _____

A perfect score is 100! How many did you get right?

Roosevelt _____

Sakakawea _____

sauerkraut _____

Sioux _____

Walhalla _____

Naturally North Dakota!

Fill in the bubblegram with some North Dakota crops and natural resources. Use the letter clues to help you.

WORD BANK
Durum wheat
Lignite coal
Livestock
Oil
Spring wheat
Sugar beets
Sunflowers

1. L _ _ ◯ ◯ _ _ C ◯ _ L

2. S _ _ _ N G W _ _ _ ◯

3. ◯ _ ◯ _ L _ W _ _ _ S

4. D _ ◯ _ _ W _ ◯ _ _ T

5. _ _ G ◯ _ B _ _ T _

6. L _ ◯ _ S _ _ ◯ K

7. ◯ _ L

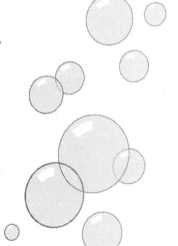

**Now unscramble the "bubble" letters to find out the mystery word!
HINT: What is one way we can help to save our environment?**

— — — — — — — — — — — —

Bonanza Farming Brings Bucks and People!

Charles Cavileer may have started the first permanent farming community in North Dakota in 1851, but farming didn't bring people to North Dakota until the 1870s.

After the railroads arrived in the state, the Red River Valley started supplying wheat to the growing milling businesses in Minnesota. A new milling process was also developed for spring wheat, a northern crop planted in the spring and harvested in the fall before the ground freezes. Flour made from the spring wheat was considered better than flour made from winter wheat. Spring wheat became the main crop of the northern plains.

Businessmen such as George W. Cass and Benjamin Cheney bought thousands of acres of land and began the first bonanza farm. Newspapers and magazines printed articles about the bonanza farms. Thousands of settlers came to North Dakota to work on the huge farms or start their own smaller farms.

The days of bonanza farming ended by 1890, but the settlers remained and farming is still important to North Dakota's economy.

Put these items in alphabetical order from 1-10.

_____ milling
_____ community
_____ bonanza
_____ economy
_____ magazines
_____ winter wheat
_____ newspapers
_____ flour
_____ northern
_____ spring wheat

ANSWERS: 1-bonanza; 2-community; 3-economy; 4-flour; 5-magazines; 6-milling; 7-newspapers; 8-northern; 9-spring wheat; 10-winter wheat

What a Great Idea!

Fill in the blanks with the choices in the Word Bank.

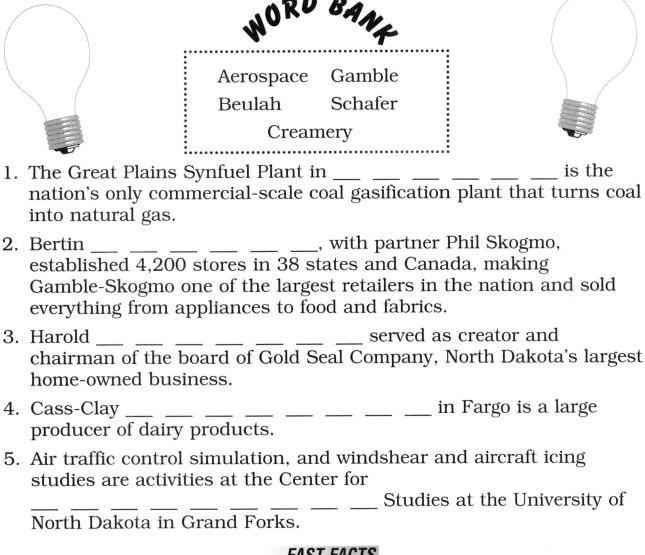

WORD BANK

Aerospace   Gamble

Beulah   Schafer

Creamery

1. The Great Plains Synfuel Plant in __ __ __ __ __ __ is the nation's only commercial-scale coal gasification plant that turns coal into natural gas.

2. Bertin __ __ __ __ __ __, with partner Phil Skogmo, established 4,200 stores in 38 states and Canada, making Gamble-Skogmo one of the largest retailers in the nation and sold everything from appliances to food and fabrics.

3. Harold __ __ __ __ __ __ __ served as creator and chairman of the board of Gold Seal Company, North Dakota's largest home-owned business.

4. Cass-Clay __ __ __ __ __ __ __ __ in Fargo is a large producer of dairy products.

5. Air traffic control simulation, and windshear and aircraft icing studies are activities at the Center for __ __ __ __ __ __ __ __ Studies at the University of North Dakota in Grand Forks.

FAST FACTS

Harold Schafer is founder of the Theodore Roosevelt Medora Foundation, the organization that owns and operates the majority of attractions in Medora.

ANSWERS: 1–Beulah; 2–Gamble; 3–Schafer; 4–Creamery; 5–Aerospace

Famous North Dakotan Scavenger Hunt!

Here is a list of some of the famous people associated with our state. **Go on a scavenger hunt to see if you can "capture" a fact about each one. Use an encyclopedia, almanac, or other resource you might need. Happy hunting!**

Dr. Robert H. Bahmer _____

Kent Conrad _____

Ronald N. Davies _____

Angie Dickinson _____

Ivan Dmitre _____

Byron L. Dorgan _____

William H. Gass _____

Reverend Richard C. Halverson _____

John Hoeven _____

Phil D. Jackson _____

Louis L'Amour _____

William Lemke _____

Roger Maris _____

Casper Oimoen _____

Cliff "Fido" Purpur _____

Eric Sevareid _____

Edward K. Thompson _____

Tommy Tucker _____

Lawrence Welk _____

Bobby Vee _____

How Devils Lake Became Salty!

Use the words in the word bank to fill in the blanks in this North Dakota legend. Some may be used more than once.

WORD BANK

attack
fish
medicine
monster
river
salty
water

Years ago a sea __ __ __ __ __ __ __ killed an army of Native Americans! After the __ __ __ __ __ __ __ appeared, the water in Devils Lake became __ __ __ __ __, and the fish disappeared.

A __ __ __ __ __ __ __ __ man named Ke-ask-ke was sent to investigate. Ke-ask-ke found an old Sioux __ __ __ __ __ __ __ __ __ man who told him this story.

The Sioux planned to __ __ __ __ __ __ the Chippewas and drive them to Canada. The Great Spirit Man appeared and told them if they did as they planned, a huge sea __ __ __ __ __ __ __ would swallow them. Just as they were ready to __ __ __ __ __ __, an ugly __ __ __ __ __ __ __ came out of the water and swallowed the Sioux, one by one. Some got away. Afterward, the water became salty and the __ __ __ __ disappeared.

The __ __ __ __ __ __ __ __ men investigated. The __ __ __ __ __ became stormy and large bubbles appeared. One of the medicine men fell out of the boat and disappeared. When he returned, he told the others he found a hole where the __ __ __ __ __ came out boiling. It led to a passage that connected to an underground __ __ __ __ __ that went to the Gulf of Mexico. They decided that was how the sea __ __ __ __ __ __ __ came to Devils Lake. All the __ __ __ __ were drawn into the __ __ __ __ __ and couldn't get back to the lake.

Map of North America

This is a map of North America. North Dakota is one of the 50 states.

Color the state of North Dakota red.

Color the rest of the United States yellow. Alaska and Hawaii are part of the United States and should also be colored yellow.

Color Canada green. Color Mexico blue.

Escarpments are ridges or cliffs that mark the boundary of a plateau (a hill or mountain with a flat top).

In the Badlands of the Missouri Plateau, erosion near rivers has shaped the land surrounding the river into buttes, or peaks, surrounded by gullies and ravines.

North Dakota's topography has three regions marked by escarpments that mark the changing elevations.

North Dakota's regions are the Red River Valley, the Drift Prairie, and the Missouri Plateau.

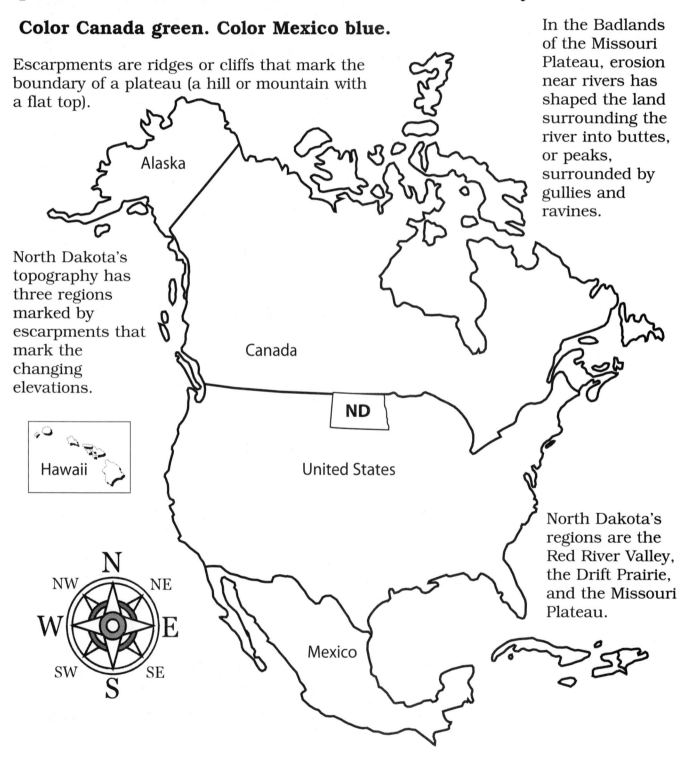

Voting in North Dakota!

True or False?!

North Dakota is the only state in the nation that doesn't require voter registration! Most states require that new voters, those who have just become old enough or have recently moved, register prior to an election. When a voter registers, his or her name is added to the list of qualified voters. In most states, voters must register at least 30 days before an election. Some states, like Minnesota, register people on the same day as the election.

The North Dakota legislature abolished voter registration in 1951. The state has many small election precincts, so local elections officials know those who come to vote on Election Day. Cities and towns can register voters for local elections, but only Medora requires it.

Qualified voters in North Dakota must be U.S. citizens, be at least 18 on Election Day, be legal state residents, and must have lived in the precinct for at least 30 days prior to the election.

Read each sentence, and decide if it is TRUE or FALSE. Write your answers on the lines provided.

1. North Dakota voters must be at least 21 on Election Day.

   _____

2. North Dakota voters must register to vote before Election Day.

   _____

3. The North Dakota legislature abolished voter registration in 1951.

   _____

4. North Dakota voters must live in their precinct at least 30 days before the election.

   _____

5. North Dakota voters don't have to be U.S. citizens.

   _____

ANSWERS: 1–false; 2–false; 3–true; 4–true; 5–false

North Dakota State Greats!

In the paragraph about important people from North Dakota below there are eight misspelled words. Circle the misspelled words, and then spell them correctly on the lines provided.

Casper Oimoen of Minot was captian of the U.S. Olympic ski team in 1936. He won more than 400 medals and trophies as a skier. He was also a bricklayer and worked with the consturction crew that built the North Dakota capital building. Roger Maris of Fargo was baseball's home run king from 1961-1998 when Mark McGwire broke his recurd. Maris hit 61 home runs during the 1961 seeson while playing for the New York Yankees.

Phil Jackson of Williston played basketball for the New York Knicks before becoming a coach. While he was coach of the Chicago Bulls, Jackson lead the team to six national championships in nine years. Boxer Virgil Hill grew up in Grand Forks and Williston. In 1987, Hill won the World Boxing Association light-heavywieght title. Cliff "Fido" Purpur was the first North Dakotan to play professional ice hockee. He has been named to the Sports Hall of Fame and the U.S. Hockey Hall of Fame.

_____   _____

_____   _____

_____   _____

_____   _____

ANSWERS: captain; construction; capitol; record; season; led; heavyweight; hockey

Virtual
North Dakota!

It's time to build your own website! We've given you pictures of things that have to do with North Dakota. Color and cut them out, and arrange them on a blank piece of paper to create a web page that will make people want to visit North Dakota!

Furs and Explorers

The exploration of North Dakota started because of furs. French explorers were the first to journey to North Dakota and build trading posts. Beaver and buffalo skins were valued. The Hudson's Bay Company from Canada was trading regularly with North Dakota's Native Americans by the 1780s.

The demand for furs grew because of European fashions. Hats made from beaver pelts were especially prized. Explorers were looking for new regions where they could find an abundance of wild animals to trap for furs.

As the fur trading business grew, the companies established trading posts and settlements throughout North Dakota. Native Americans started working for the companies as hired trappers.

Many of the early French traders married Cree and Chippewa women. Their children were called *Métis*. The Métis developed the Red River cart which was used to carry goods, such as buffalo skins, across the prairie. Red River carts had two high wheels and were pulled by an ox. The cart could carry a 1,000-pound (454-kilogram) load across the uneven prairie sod.

Read each sentence, and decide what is the CAUSE and what is the EFFECT. Find the cause and effect parts of each of the sentences below. Underline the cause once, and the effect twice.

1. The demand for furs grew because furs were fashionable in Europe.

2. The demand for furs brought explorers to North Dakota.

3. When fur trade businesses grew, the fur companies built trading posts and settlements in North Dakota.

4. When French explorers married Cree and Chippewa women, their children and descendants were called Métis.

5. To help carry goods across the prairie, the Métis designed the Red River cart.

A River Runs Through It!

The state of North Dakota is blessed with many rivers. See if you can wade right in and figure out these rivers' names! **For each river code, circle every other letter (beginning with the second one) to discover the name!**

WORD BANK

CANNONBALL
HEART
KNIFE
MISSOURI
RED RIVER OF THE NORTH
RUSH

---

1. This river "cuts" a path through Beulah and Hazen and shares its name with a national historic site.

   D K G N J I K F L E

2. During pioneer days, this was the ammunition used by the "big guns" at forts.

   A C R A Y N I N K O L N M B X A S L F L

3. This river is in a "hurry" to get from Erie to Reile's Acres.

   W R Q U C S B H

4. Lake Tschida is found on this river that has a "beat."

   R H Y E U A P R K T

5. This river enters North Dakota from Montana at the Fort Union National Historic Site and flows into South Dakota after passing through the Standing Rock Indian Reservation.

   S M F I H S K S L O M U V R X I

6. This river separates North Dakota from Minnesota.

   A R G E F D   H R J I K V L E U R   B O V F   C T X H Z E

   W N R O P R K T S H

North Dakota Firsts!

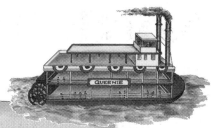

The World's Largest Quilt Creation!
It took 7,000 North Dakota residents to make the world's largest quilt for the North Dakota Centennial in 1989. The quilt measures 85 feet x 135 feet (26 meters x 41 meters).

First Steamboat Chugs to North Dakota!
The *Yellowstone* was the first steamboat to run on the upper Missouri River in 1832. The boat traveled to Fort Union, the junction of the Yellowstone and Missouri rivers.

Read All About It!
North Dakota's first newspaper, *The Frontier Scout*, began publication at Fort Union in 1864.

Here Comes the Judge!
Beryl Leaven was named the first woman justice on the North Dakota Supreme Court in 1985.

North Dakota is #1!
North Dakota is first in the nation in the production of spring wheat, durum wheat, sunflowers, barley, all dry edible beans, pinto beans, canola, and flaxseed.

Hamburger Heaven!
The town of Rutland went into the Guinness Book of World Records in 1982 when it cooked and ate the world's largest hamburger. Between 8,000-10,000 people helped eat the 3,591-pound (1,629-kilogram) hamburger.

Which "first" happened first?
The *Yellowstone* is the first steamboat to reach Fort Union.
North Dakota's first newspaper is published.
North Dakota residents make the world's largest quilt.

ANSWER: The *Yellowstone* is the first steamboat to reach Fort Union

North Dakota Gazetteer

A gazetteer is a list of places. For each of these famous North Dakota places, write down the town in which it's located, and one interesting fact about the place. You may have to use an encyclopedia, almanac, or other resource to find the information, so dig deep!

1. World's Largest Buffalo Statue _____
   _____

2. Abbey Church _____
   _____

3. International Peace Garden
   _____
   _____

4. Bonanzaville, U.S.A.
   _____
   _____

5. Garrison Dam _____
   _____

6. Geographic Center of North America Pioneer Village and Museum _____
   _____

7. Pembina State Historic Site _____
   _____

8. De Mores State Historic Site _____
   _____

WORD BANK

Dunseith	Pembina	Rugby
Jamestown	Richardton	West Fargo
Medora	Riverdale	

A Settler Corn Husk Doll

You can make a corn husk doll similar to the dolls
North Dakota settlers' children played with!
Here's how:

You will need:
- corn husks (or strips of cloth)
- string
- scissors

1. **Select a long piece of corn husk and fold it in half. Tie a string about one inch (2.54 centimeters) down from the fold to make the doll's head.**

2. **Roll a husk and put it between the layers of the tied husk, next to the string. Tie another string around the longer husk, just below the rolled husk. Now your doll has arms! Tie short pieces of string at the ends of the rolled husk to make the doll's hands.**

3. **Make your doll's waist by tying another string around the longer husk.**

4. **If you want your doll to have legs, cut the longer husk up the middle. Tie the two halves at the bottom to make feet.**

5. **Add eyes and a nose to your doll with a marker. You could use corn silk for the doll's hair.**

Now you can make a whole family of dolls!

North Dakota Timeline!

A timeline is a list of important events and the year that they happened. You can use a timeline to understand more about history.

Read the timeline about Utah history, then see if you can answer the questions at the bottom.

1738   Pierre Gaultier de Varennes, Sieur de La Vérendrye, is the first person to write an account of his travels through North Dakota

1801   Alexander Henry the Younger establishes trading post at Pembina for the North West Company

1804   Meriwether Lewis and William Clark Expedition builds winter quarters in North Dakota and hires Toussaint Charbonneau and his wife, Sakakawea, as guides

1837   Smallpox epidemic nearly destroys the Mandan Indians

1868   Major peace council between the United States and the Sioux results in the Laramie Treaty and gives the Sioux a reservation west of the Missouri River

1872   Railroad reaches the Red River

1883   Bismarck becomes capital of the Dakota Territory

1889   Enabling Act divides Dakota Territory into two states; North Dakota admitted to the Union as the 39th state

1932   International Peace Garden is dedicated

1951   Oil is discovered near Tioga; voter registration law is repealed, North Dakota becomes only state without this requirement

Now put yourself back in the proper year if you were the following people.

1. If you are excited because the International Peace Garden has been dedicated, the year is _____.

2. If you decide to seek your fortune as an oil prospector near Tioga, the year is _____.

3. If you heard that someone has written about their travels through North Dakota, the year is _____.

4. If you are happy because North Dakota has become a state, the year is _____.

5. If you are planning to take your first train to North Dakota's Red River from the east, the year is _____.

6. If you decide to move to Bismarck because it became the territorial capital, the year is _____.

7. If you have decided to trade at the trading post built by Alexander Henry the Younger, the year is _____.

8. If you are upset that smallpox caused your Mandan Indian friend to die, the year is _____.

ANSWERS: 1-1932; 2-1951; 3-1738; 4-1889; 5-1872; 6-1883; 7-1801; 8-1837

North Dakota State Economy!

North Dakota banks provide essential financial services.
Some of the services that banks provide include:

- They lend money to consumers to purchase goods and services such as houses, cars, and education.
- They lend money to producers who start new businesses.
- They issue credit cards.
- They provide savings accounts and pay interest to savers.
- They provide checking accounts.

Circle whether you would have more, less, or the same amount of money after each event.

1. You deposit your paycheck into your checking account. MORE   LESS   SAME

2. You put $1,000 in your savings account. MORE   LESS   SAME

3. You use your credit card to buy new school clothes. MORE   LESS   SAME

4. You borrow money from the bank to open a toy store. MORE   LESS   SAME

5. You write a check at the grocery store. MORE   LESS   SAME

6. You transfer money from checking to savings. MORE   LESS   SAME

North Dakota is a right to work state, which means workers do not have to belong to a union as a condition of employment.

Most North Dakotans work in the service industry.

ANSWERS: 1–more; 2–more; 3–less; 4–more; 5–less; 6–same

I Am A Famous Person From North Dakota

From the Word Bank, find my name and fill in the blank.

WORD BANK

James B. Power

Father Sévère Dumoulin

Manuel Lisa

Pierre Gaultier de Varennes,
Sieur de La Vérendrye

David Thompson

George Armstrong Custer

1. I was stationed at Fort Abraham Lincoln in North Dakota. I was killed at the Battle of Little Big Horn in Montana.
   Who am I? _____   _____

2. I was a fur trader who built several trading posts on the Missouri River. I was known for my fair treatment of the Indians I traded with.
   Who am I? _____   _____

3. I was a Roman Catholic missionary and I worked with Father Joseph Provencher. I opened the first church in North Dakota at Pembina.
   Who am I? _____   _____

4. I worked for the Hudson's Bay Company and the North West Company. I made the first map of North Dakota.
   Who am I? _____   _____

5. I am called the "father of bonanza farming." I convinced George Cass and Benjamin Cheney to start the first bonanza farm.
   Who am I? _____   _____

6. I was trying to find a water route to the Pacific Ocean. I was the first European known to come to North Dakota.
   Who am I? _____   _____

ANSWERS: 1–George Armstrong Custer; 2–Manuel Lisa; 3–Father Sévère Dumoulin; 4–David Thompson; 5–James B. Power; 6–Pierre Gaultier de Varennes, Sieur de La Vérendrye

Mounds Abound in North Dakota!

North Dakota is home to several historic Indian sites. Ruins of earth lodge dwellings built by the Mandans are found at the Huff Indian Village State Historic Site near Huff. Medicine Rock State Historic Site in Grant County is an area of religious importance to Native Americans. The earth lodge village at the Menoken Indian Village State Historic Site is surrounded by a fortification ditch. Pulver Mounds State Historic Site has the remains of two low burial grounds from the Woodland Culture.

You are an archaeologist digging at the Menoken Indian Village State Historic Site. Below are pictures of some of the artifacts that you find. Now, you have to identify these strange objects and their uses. **Write down what you think these things are for!**

_____ _____ _____ _____

_____ _____ _____ _____

_____ _____ _____ _____

North Dakota Native Americans!

When the explorers arrived in North Dakota, there were several Native American groups already living there. **Draw a line from each group to its location on the map.**

    The Mandan, Hidatsas, and Arikaras made their homes in permanent villages along the Missouri River. The Chippewas lived in the forests of the Turtle and Pembina mountains. The Objibwa lived in the northeast, and the Assiniboine were found in the northwest. The Sioux, which included several different groups, were found in southeast and southwest North Dakota.

    As more settlers came to North Dakota, the Indians were pushed off the lands where they had lived for decades. Government treaties promised the tribes land, food, supplies, and that no settlers would be allowed on the reservations. But as more settlers came, the government forgot the treaties. Fighting broke out in 1862 and continued until 1876 when the last of the Sioux were confined to reservations.

Mandan   Ojibwa

Hidatsa   Assiniboine

Arikara   Chippewa

Sioux

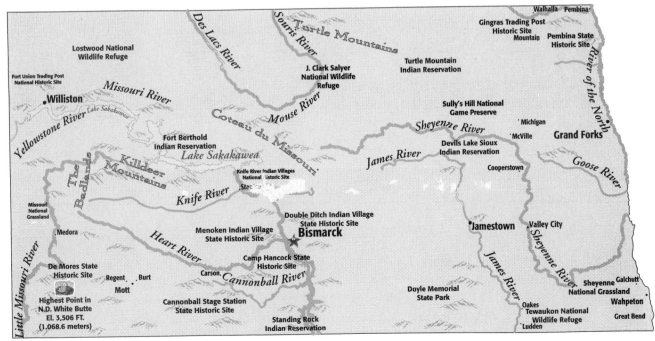

IT'S MONEY IN THE BANK!!

You spent the summer working at Cass-Clay Creamery in Fargo, and you made a lot of money...$500 to be exact!
Solve the math problems below.

TOTAL EARNED: $500.00

I will pay back my Mom this much
for money I borrowed when I first
started working. Thanks, Mom!   A. $20.00

    subtract A from $500   B. _____

I will give my little brother this much
money for taking my phone messages
while I was at work: C. $10.00

    subtract C from B   D. _____

I will spend this much on a special
treat or reward for myself: E. $25.00

    subtract E from D   F. _____

I will save this much for college: G. $300.00

    subtract G from F   H. _____

I will put this much in my new
savings account so I can buy school   I. $100.00
clothes:

    subtract I from H   J. _____

TOTAL STILL AVAILABLE
       (use answer J)   _____

TOTAL SPENT   (add A, C, and E)   _____

Alice Ate Wild Rice on the Beach!

Find these North Dakota cities and towns in the word search!

ALICE
ALFRED
ANTLER
BEACH
BLOOM
CANNONBALL
CONCRETE
HOPE

MICHIGAN
MOUNTAIN
NEW ENGLAND
RUGBY
WHEATLAND
WILD RICE
ZAP

```
K N O A L I C E R T H K A K O
A O T A L W H E A T L A N D K
D N O R T F M I C H I G A N A
H H D A M K R O T A N O R E D
T T K O A U E K O A T A W H
R N O R O T G H D D N A K E T
O O T A L N B O R T T H D N R
N A K O B T Y A N O L R T G O
A H N O R E T H E D E A K L N
T O T A N O A R P T R H L A D
O D A K O T A C O N O A R N T
K T H D A K O U H T B A N D O
A O R T H N K M W N A K O T K
D A N O C R T I O H D A K O A
H T A R N O L N R U T H D A D
T K E O T D N A N O N R T H H
R T D A R A K O T A N T O Z T
E R T I C H D A K O T A A N R
O O C R T H D A K O T P A I O
N E N O R T H D A K O T A N N
```

©2001 Carole Marsh/Gallopade International/800-536-2GET/www.northdakotaexperience.com/Page 75

Numbering the North Dakotans!

STATE OF NORTH DAKOTA
CENSUS REPORT

Every ten years, it's time for North Dakotans to stand up and be counted. Since 1790, the United States has conducted a census, or count, of each of its citizens. **Practice filling out a pretend census form.**

Name _____ Age [ ]

Place of Birth _____

Current Address _____

Does your family own or rent where you live? _____

How long have you lived in North Dakota? _____

How many people are in your family? _____

How many females? [ ]   How many males? [ ]

What are their ages? _____

How many rooms are in your house? [ ]

How is your home heated? _____

How many cars does your family own? [ ]

How many telephones are in your home? [ ]

Is your home a farm? _____

Sounds pretty nosy, doesn't it? But a census is very important. The information is used for all kinds of purposes, including setting budgets, zoning land, determining how many schools to build, and much more. The census helps North Dakota leaders plan for the future needs of its citizens. Hey, that's you!!

Endangered and Threatened North Dakota

Each state has a list of the endangered species found within its borders. An animal is labeled endangered when it is at risk of becoming extinct, or dying out completely. Land development, changes in climate and weather, and changes in the number of predators are all factors that can cause an animal to become extinct. Today many states are passing laws to help save animals on the endangered species list.

1. W H __ __ __ I __ __   C __ A __ __

2. E __ __ I __ __   C __ __ L __ __

3. B __ __ D E A __ __ E

4. B __ __ __ __ -F __ __ T __ __   F E __ __ E __

5. P __ __ I __ __   P __ O __ __ R

6. P A __ __ I __   S __ U __ __ E __ __

7. L __ __ __ T T __ __ N

8. __ __ A __ W __ __ F

Circle the animal that is extinct (not here anymore).

Singing North Dakota's Praises!

North Dakota Hymn
Words by James W. Foley
Music arranged by Dr. C.S. Putnam

North Dakota, North Dakota
With thy prairies wide and free,
All thy sons and daughters love thee,
Fairest state from sea to sea;
North Dakota, North Dakota,
Here we pledge ourselves to thee.
North Dakota, North Dakota,
Here we pledge ourselves to thee.

Hear thy loyal children singing,
Songs of happiness and praise,
Far and long the echoes ringing
Through the vastness of thy ways-
North Dakota, North Dakota,
We will serve thee all our days.
North Dakota, North Dakota,
We will serve thee all our days.

Answer the following questions:

1. What kind of prairies are in North Dakota?

_____

2. What kinds of songs do North Dakota's children sing?

_____

3. Who loves North Dakota?

_____

4. What will we (North Dakota residents) do all our days?

_____

ANSWERS: (may vary slightly) 1–wide and free; 2–songs of happiness and praise; 3–all of North Dakota's sons and daughters; 4–serve North Dakota

Getting Ready To Vote in North Dakota

When you turn 18, you will be eligible to vote. Your vote counts! Many elections have been won by just a few votes. **The following is a form for your personal voting information. You will need to do some research to get all the answers!**

I will be eligible to vote on this date _____

I live in this Congressional District _____

I live in this State Senate District _____

I live in this State Representative District _____

I live in this Voting Precinct _____

The first local election I can vote in will be _____

The first state election I can vote in will be _____

The first national election I can vote in will be _____

The governor of our state is _____

One of my state senators is _____

One of my state representatives is _____

The local public office I would like to run for is _____

The state public office I would like to run for is _____

The federal public office I would like to run for is _____

Did you know that our state government has 53 senators?

The number of legislators may change after each census.

No, but I do know we have 106 representatives!

North Dakota State Seal

The state seal of North Dakota features a tree in an open field, its trunk surrounded by bundles of wheat. A plow, an anvil, a sledge, a bow with three arrows, and an Indian on horseback chasing a buffalo toward the setting sun stand for the work and history of North Dakota. A half-circle of 42 stars stands for the number of states in the Union in 1889.

Color the state seal.

North Dakota State Symbol Scramble!

Unscramble the names of these symbols for the state of North Dakota. Write the answers in the word wheel around the picture of each symbol.

1. W D L I   R I P E R A I   R E S O
   Hint: It grows along roads, in pastures, and in native meadows and produces a fruit called rose hip.

2. T A K O N O   S O H R E
   Hint: It is found in the Theodore Roosevelt National Park and may be related to Chief Sitting Bull's horse.

3. R N O E R T H N   I E K P
   Hint: It has a long body and flat snout and is found in the rivers and lakes of North Dakota.

4. E A M A C N I R   M L E
   Hint: It grows more than 100 feet (30 meters) tall, and it loses its leaves in the fall.

5. D E E R O T   E T I E P F R I D   D O W O
   Hint: It was a worm-shaped mollusk that lived in trees more than 50 million years ago.

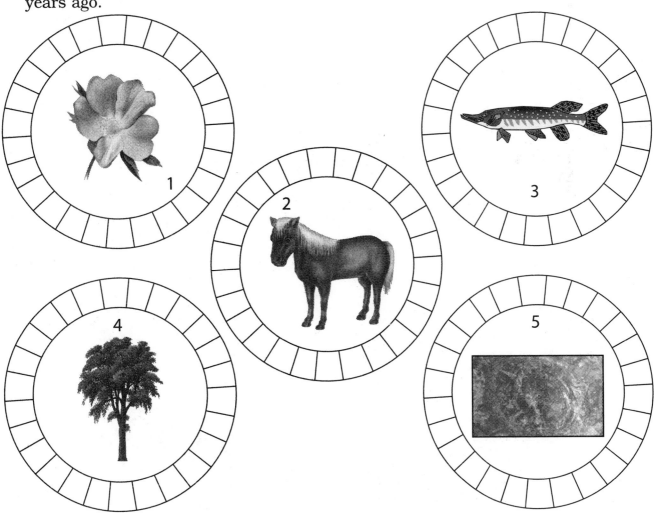

A Quilt Of Many Counties

North Dakota has 53 counties

  North Dakota's county governments take care of the administrative and business affairs at the local level. An elected board of commissioners governs the counties. Other elected county offices include sheriff, treasurer, and auditor.

- **Label your county. Color it red.**
- **Label the counties that touch your county. Color them blue.**
- **Now color the rest of the counties green.**

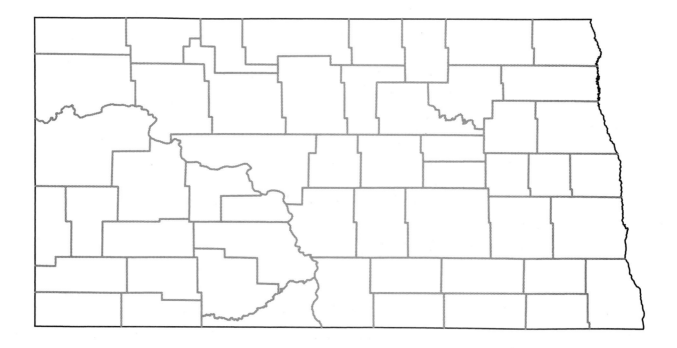

It's Time to Celebrate!

Nordic food, arts and crafts, and big-name entertainers are featured at the Norsk Hostfest held every fall in Minot. More than 60,000 Norwegians and non-Norwegians alike attend the annual ethnic celebration. North Dakota residents with German roots hold their own Oktoberfest celebrations. In October, the town of Wishek honors the fermented cabbage dish called sauerkraut with Sauerkraut Days. School gets out early so the students can enjoy the free weiner-and-kraut lunch served during the festival. If sauerkraut is not your dish, you can try *knoephla* soup or *pierogi*.

North Dakota has many great celebrations! Visit these North Dakota events to answer the questions below.

- Homefest, Watford City
- Buffalo Trails Day, Williston
- Fort Union Rendezvous
- Roughrider Days Rodeo, Dickinson
- Frontier Army Days, Fort Abraham Lincoln
- Cannon Ball Powwow, Standing Rock Reservation
- Porcupine Powwow, Shields
- Norsk Hostfest, Minot
- North Dakota State Fair, Minot
- International Ragtop Festival, Rolla
- Pioneer Days, Fargo
- Sheyenne Arts and Crafts Festival, Fort Ransom
- Fort Seward Wagon Train, Jamestown
- Sauerkraut Days, Wishek
- Medora Musical

1. Parades and rock 'n roll concerts are among the activities that pay homage to the __ __ __ __ __ __ __ __ __ __ __ at the International Ragtop Festival.
2. The life of our country's 26th president,

   __ __ __ __ __ __ __ __ __ __

   __ __ __ __ __ __ __ __ __ __, is celebrated at the Medora Musical every summer.
3. Rodeos, parades, tractor pulls, and carnival rides can be found at the North Dakota State Fair in __ __ __ __ __ .
4. Wear your period costumes to __ __ __ __ __ __ __ Days in Fargo!

ANSWERS: 1–convertible; 2–Theodore Roosevelt; 3–Minot; 4–Pioneer

Farmers Fight for a Fair Share!

The Nonpartisan League (NPL) was a political **organization** that formed in North Dakota in 1915. During the early 1900s, North Dakota's farmers felt they weren't getting their fair share of the **profits** made by the people who bought their crops, then sold the crops to mills and stores. The farmers tried to work together and formed associations to try to get a fair market price for their product. They weren't very **successful.**

As a result, Arthur C. Townley, a former farmer, decided a larger, more powerful group was needed. He formed the NPL. Within a year, the NPL had 40,000 members. The NPL believed state ownership of grain elevators, flour mills, and banks would solve the problems. A state-owned bank opened in 1919. The state also opened a mill and elevator in 1922. The bank, mill, and elevator are still in **operation**. The NPL was powerful in North Dakota **politics** for many years. By the 1930s, the NPL had lost most of its power because of **disagreements** among the members and the Depression.

See if you can figure out the meanings of these words from the story above.

1. organization _____

2. profit _____

3. successful _____

4. operation _____

5. politics _____

6. disagreements

_____

Now check your answers in a dictionary. How close did you get to the real definitions?

Which Founding Person Am I?

From the Word Bank, find my name and fill in the blank.

WORD BANK

Pierre Bottineau   Charles Chaboillez

Charles Cavileer   John Miller

Antoine de Vallombrosa,
the Marquis de Mores

Alexander Henry the Younger

1. I built the first trading post to be located entirely within North Dakota at Pembina in 1797. I was a fur trader for the North West Company.
   Who am I? _____

2. I built a trading post built at Pembina in 1801. It became the center of the first settlement in North Dakota.
   Who am I? _____

3. I was a French nobleman and businessman who founded the town of Medora. I built a ranch, a meat-packing plant, and started a stagecoach service.
   Who am I? _____

4. I influenced people to come to North Dakota. I was the leader of the first permanent farming community in Pembina.
   Who am I? _____

5. I was a political leader. I was elected to the Dakota Territorial Council in 1888 and became the state's first governor in 1889.
   Who am I? _____

6. I was a Métis leader in the Red River Valley. I led many expeditions across the northern plains.
   Who am I? _____

ANSWERS: 1– Charles Chaboillez; 2– Alexander Henry the Younger; 3–Antoine de Vallombrosa, the Marquis de Mores; 4–Charles Cavileer; 5–John Miller; 6–Pierre Bottineau

!! It Could Happen— And It Did! !!

These historical events from North Dakota's past are all out of order. Can you put them back together in the correct order? Number these events from 1 to 10, beginning with the earliest. (There's a great big hint at the end of each sentence.)

_____ Oil is discovered near Tioga (1951)

_____ Railroad reaches the Red River (1872)

_____ North Dakota opens for homesteading under the Homestead Act of 1862 (1863)

_____ René-Robert Cavelier, Sieur de La Salle, claims the territory known as Louisiana (including a large part of North Dakota) for France (1682)

_____ A treaty with Great Britain gives the United States the rest of present-day North Dakota (1818)

_____ Alexander Henry the Younger establishes trading post at Pembina for the North West Company (1801)

_____ Bill legalizing homeschooling is passed by the legislature (1989)

_____ Thomas Douglas, Earl of Selkirk, sends Scottish and Irish settlers to establish settlement at Pembina (1812)

_____ Theodore Roosevelt National Park is created (1947)

_____ Pierre Gaultier de Varennes, Sieur de La Vérendrye, is the first person to write an account of his travels through North Dakota (1738)

ANSWERS: 9; 7; 6; 1; 5; 3; 10; 4; 8; 2

Cattle and Cowboys!

Cattle ranching was introduced to the western Dakota Territory in the late 1870s. The Badlands became known as a cattle-grazing region. One of the many ranchers who came to North Dakota was Theodore Roosevelt. Roosevelt was part owner of the Maltese Cross Ranch and later purchased the Elkhorn Ranch.

Cowboys worked on the ranches. Rodeos developed as a way for the cowboys to show off their skills, as well as compete against each other. Cowboys, and cowgirls, are still a big part of North Dakota. Rodeos and frontier days festivals held throughout the state celebrate cowboys and their contribution to North Dakota's history.

Here's a cowboy gettin' ready to ride! Label the parts of his clothing, using the Word Bank below.

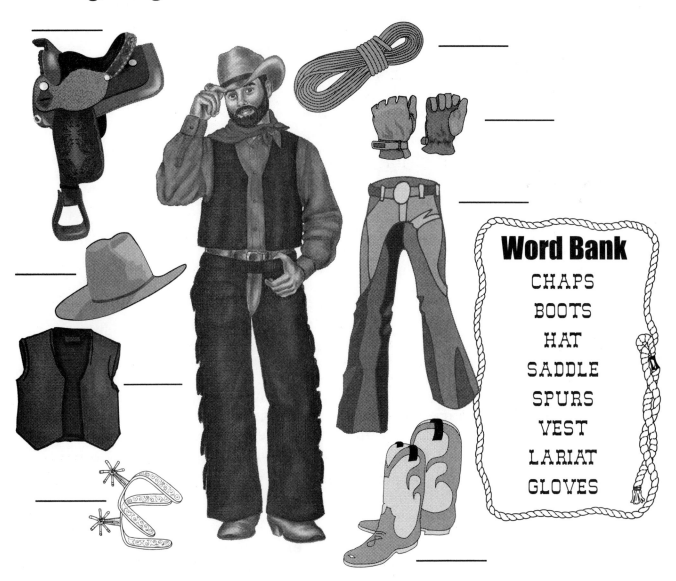

Word Bank

CHAPS
BOOTS
HAT
SADDLE
SPURS
VEST
LARIAT
GLOVES

Notable North Dakotans!

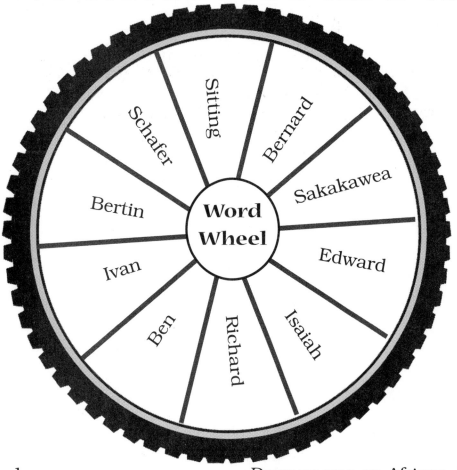

Word Wheel

Schafer · Sitting · Bernard · Sakakawea · Edward · Isaiah · Richard · Ben · Ivan · Bertin

Using the Word Wheel of North Dakota names, complete the sentences below.

1. __ __ __ __ __ __ Dorman was an African-American frontiersman who served as the Sioux interpreter at Fort Rice until he was killed at the Battle of the Little Big Horn in Montana.

2. Sculptor John __ __ __ __ __ __ __ Flannagan was born in Fargo and is best known for his animal sculptures.

3. __ __ __ __ __ __ __ Bull, the legendary Sioux chief, was killed at the Standing Rock Indian Reservation.

4. __ __ __ __ __ __ __ K. Thompson served as editor of *Life* magazine from 1937-1968 and was the first editor and publisher of the *Smithsonian* magazine from 1969-1981.

5. __ __ __ __ Dmitri was a well-known photographer and artist who was also known as Levon West.

6. Carl __ __ __ Eielson of Hatton was an aviator and explorer who co-piloted the first airplane to cross the Arctic Ocean.

7. __ __ __ __ __ __ C. Gamble and his partner established one of the largest department store chains in the United States.

8. Harold __ __ __ __ __ __ __ founded North Dakota's largest home-owned business, Gold Seal Company.

9. Reverend __ __ __ __ __ __ __ C. Halverson served as the U.S. Senate chaplain.

10. __ __ __ __ __ __ __ __ __ and her son are remembered with a statue on the grounds of the North Dakota state capitol building.

ANSWERS: 1-Isaiah; 2-Bernard; 3-Sitting; 4-Edward; 5-Ivan; 6-Ben; 7-Bertin; 8-Schafer; 9-Richard; 10-Sakakawea

North Dakota Pop Quiz!

**Pop quiz! It's time to test your knowledge of North Dakota!
Try to answer all of the questions before
you look at the answers.**

1. North Dakota's nickname is
   a) the Gem State
   b) the Sunshine State
   c) the Peace Garden State

2. North Dakota became the 39th state in
   a) 1889
   b) 1863
   c) 1781

3. North Dakota's state capital is
   a) Pierre
   b) Bismarck
   c) Helena

4. North Dakota's state beverage is
   a) milk
   b) apple juice
   c) cranberry juice

5. North Dakota's highest point is
   a) Mount Rainier
   b) White Butte
   c) Mount Rushmore

6. North Dakota's largest rivers are
   a) the Missouri and Red River of the North
   b) Pembina and Goose
   c) Sheyenne and James

7. The geographic center of North America is located in
   a) Cando
   b) Rugby
   c) Streeter

8. North Dakota's state grass is
   a) bermuda
   b) bluebunch wheatgrass
   c) western wheatgrass

9. North Dakota's state tree is the
   a) Douglas fir
   b) American elm
   c) Ponderosa pine

10. The largest natural body of water in North Dakota is
    a) Lake Sakakawea
    b) Long Lake
    c) Devils Lake

ANSWERS: 1-c; 2-a; 3-b; 4-a; 5-b; 6-a; 7-b; 8-c; 9-c; 10-c

Nurturing Nokota Horses!

Nokota horses once ran wild in the Little Missouri Badlands in southwest North Dakota. Their history goes back to the warhorses taken by the U.S. government from Chief Sitting Bull and the Sioux in 1881. About 350 horses were sold to local traders, who then sold 250 mares to the Marquis de Mores, founder of the town of Medora. De Mores planned to breed the mares, many of which were warhorses. Most of de Mores' Nokotas were sold. The rest were left in the wild in the area that became the Theodore Roosevelt National Park.

In the years that followed, the state and federal agencies tried to get rid of the wild horses in western North Dakota. Eventually, the agencies decided to kill, or remove, the Nokota stallions and replaced them with other breeds. Leo and Frank Kuntz bought some of the horses that were rounded up and decided to save the breed. They have dedicated their lives to preserving the breed that is now found only on their ranch in Linton.

In 1993, the Nokota horse was designated as the honorary state equine by the state legislature.

In each pair of sentences below, one of the statements is false. Read them carefully and choose the sentence that is not true. Cross out the false sentence, and circle the true sentence.

1. The Nokota horse was chosen as the honorary state equine in 1993.
   The Nokota horse was chosen as the honorary state equine in 1983.

2. The Nokota breed can trace its history to Sitting Bull's war ponies.
   The Nokota breed can trace its history to the war ponies used by the Mandan tribe.

3. Wild Nokota horses were found on the Kuntz ranch in Linton.
   Wild Nokota horses roamed in the Theodore Roosevelt National Park.

4. The Marquis de Mores bought 250 stallions that were Sitting Bull's war ponies.
   The Marquis de Mores bought 250 mares that were Sitting Bull's war ponies.

5. The Kuntz brothers decided to save the Nokota breed.
   The Kuntz brothers tried to mix the Nokota breed with another.

ANSWERS: (Answers indicate false sentences) 1–second; 2–second; 3–first; 4–first; 5–second

Where Do North Dakotans Live?

North Dakota is the most rural of all the states. More than 90% of the state is covered with farms. Fargo is North Dakota's biggest city with a population of 90,599. Bismarck is next with 55,532. Grand Forks has a population of 49,321, and Minot boasts 36,567 residents. Smaller cities include Dickinson, 16,010; Williston, 12,512; Wahpeton, 8,586; and Valley City, 6,826. Westhope has a population of 575. Strasburg, the birthplace of Lawrence Welk, has 600 inhabitants. Fort Yates' residents number 183. Hannah's population is 20. Hansboro has 8 residents, and Maza is home to 5 people.

Using the information in the paragraphs above, graph populations of the cities listed. The first one has been done for you.

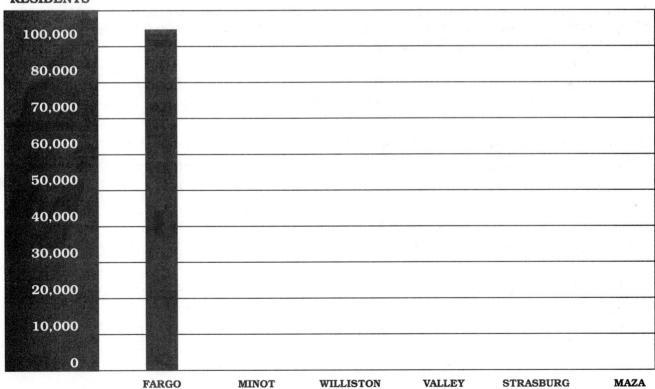

RESIDENTS

Celebrating Peace and Friendship!

The International Peace Garden celebrates the years of peace between the United States and Canada! The state of North Dakota donated 888 acres (359 hectares) for the garden and the Canadian province of Manitoba donated 1,451 acres (587 hectares). The garden is nestled in the Turtle Mountains, north of Dunseith. More than 50,000 people attended the dedication of the International Peace Garden in 1932.

The garden is located on the longest north-south road in the world and is located about an hour's drive north of Rugby, North Dakota, the geographical center of North America. More than 120,000 annuals bloom along the border between the two countries in tribute to the friendship that has lasted for years. The International Peace Garden sponsors the International Music Camp each summer, which offers courses in both the performing and visual arts. In addition, the camp sponsors the annual Old Time Fiddlers' Contest and the International Festival of the Arts.

A *haiku* is a three-line poem with a certain number of syllables in each line. Look at the example below:

> The first line has 5 syllables
> A gar/den of peace
>
> The second line has 7 syllables
> U/nit/ed States, Can/a/da,
>
> The third line has 5 syllables
> Cel/e/brate friend/ship!

Now, write your own haiku about the amazing International Peace Garden!

_____

_____

_____

World's Largest Buffalo!

The Jamestown Chamber of Commerce wanted to find a way to honor the buffalo herds that once roamed freely through the Great Plains! In 1957, the idea for a monument like other giant tourist attractions started taking shape. Jamestown College art instructor Elmer Paul Peterson designed the World's Largest Buffalo.
Nelson Rockefeller, who was governor of New York at the time, dedicated the bison statue in 1960.

The buffalo is sculpted from stucco and concrete over a steel frame. The bison is 26 feet (8 meters) high, 46 feet (14 meters) long, and 14 feet (4.2 meters) wide. It weighs 60 tons (54 metric tons).

LENGTH

HEIGHT   WIDTH   WEIGHT

How Big is North Dakota?

North Dakota is the 17th largest state in the United States. It has an area of approximately 70,704 square miles (183,109.2 square kilometers).

Can you answer the following questions?

1. How many states are there in the United States?

   _____

2. This many states are smaller than our state:

   _____

3. This many states are larger than our state:

   _____

4. One mile = 5,280 ____ ____ ____ ____

   HINT:

5. Draw a square foot.

6. Classroom Challenge: After you have drawn a square foot, measure the number of square feet in your classroom. Most floor tiles are square feet (12 inches by 12 inches). How many square feet are in your classroom? _____

   Bonus: Try to calculate how many classrooms would fit in the total area of your state. _____

   Hint: About 46,464 average classrooms would fit in just one square mile!

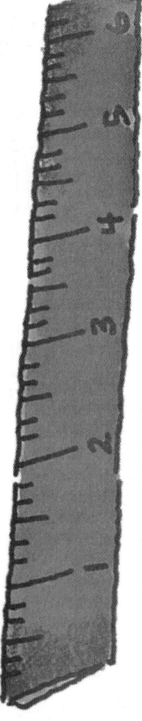

BONUS: 3,285,190,656 classrooms!

ANSWERS: 1-50; 2-33; 3-16; 4-feet

A Capital Capitol!

In 1930, North Dakota's original capitol building in Bismarck was destroyed by fire. Work on a new building began in 1933 and was completed in 1934 at a cost of $2 million. In 1981, the judicial wing was completed. It is North Dakota's tallest building at 241 feet, 8 inches (73 meters, 20 centimeters). North Dakota's capitol is one of four high-rise capitol buildings in the nation. The others are in Louisiana, Florida, and Nebraska.

The 19-story building design is Art Deco, a style of architecture popular in the 1930s and 1940s that used geometrical designs, bold colors, and bold outlines. The raw materials in the building include Indiana limestone, Montana yellowstone, Tennessee marble, Belgian marble, Honduras mahogany, East Indian rosewood, Burma teak, English brown oak, and laurel wood.

Answer the following questions based on the information provided above.

1. How tall is the North Dakota capitol building?

2. In what city is the North Dakota capitol building located.

3. How many high-rise capitol buildings are there in the United States?

4 What style of architecture is used in the North Dakota capitol building?

5. How much did it cost to build the North Dakota capitol building?

ANSWERS: 1–241 feet, 8 inches; 2–Bismarck; 3–4; 4–Art Deco; 5–$2 million

Noteworthy
North Dakota!

The words below are known as an acrostic. See if you can make up your own acrostic poem describing North Dakota. For each letter in North Dakota's name, write down a phrase that describes North Dakota. The first is done for you.

N is for   the National Buffalo Museum _____

O is for _____

R is for _____

T is for _____

H is for _____

D is for _____

A is for _____

K is for _____

O is for _____

T is for _____

A is for _____